Coaching Clients Comments

"Tony is a man of integrity and honor. He truly understands the art of coaching leaders and entrepreneurs to get them to perform at their highest level. Tony genuinely cares about his clients and their progress as leaders. He operates at the highest ethical and moral standards. You will not find someone more committed to his clients than Tony. I found something of value both professionally and personally in my coaching sessions with him. He is the best!"

Martin Noto
Executive Vice President, Chief Lending Officer
Ciera Bank

"Having Tony coach our business is like having a personal Warren Buffet, Dalai Lama, Bobby Fischer, and Vince Lombardi all together with his undivided attention. He is the single greatest human asset we have in our corner. I anticipate that we will in some form always be engaged with him in our business. In fact, if you have businesses in your portfolio that are experiencing slow growth, dis-functional ownership/management or need to organize themselves to succeed; Tony is the guy you need!"

Andrew & Lisa Fuld
Four Color Press

"Tony has been instrumental in my career growth, providing guidance and expertise that propelled me to new heights. His thought-provoking questions and unwavering support have helped me uncover my true potential. I highly recommend Tony for transformative leadership development."

Shawn Michael
President, Lon Smith Roofing

"I have known Tony for 30+ years, but really got to know him via my coaching sessions. Not only did Tony help me focus on clarity and execution of a business plan, he also taught me how to build success around an all-encompassing life plan. Taking care of my faith, family, and work plan, makes for a successful life plan. I have seen all aspects of my life improve from my time with Tony."

Craig M. Harbuck
Executive Vice President
Higginbotham

"Tony has completely changed my life; personally, professionally, and spiritually. He has guided me through some very challenging situations with grace and wisdom. Since I have been working with Tony, I have improved as a Husband, Father, Business Owner, and Christian. I value the time that I get to spend with him each week."

Jeramy Williams, Architect, NCARB
Principal Architect
JAW Architects, Inc.

"My first question when I met with Tony was – "How can I like my business again?" He helped me with this and more. Tony has a way of simplifying complex problems and issues and finding the thing behind the thing. Not only did my business satisfaction – and success – improve, but also my personal life, in ways I didn't think were connected. Tony is a continuing force in my business today and has helped my staff and me work through several difficult situations and end up much better than we started."

Gregory W. Monroe
Baker and Monroe, PLLC
Board Certified - Commercial Real Estate Law
Texas Board of Legal Specialization

* Additional comments on pages 275-276

Author's Request

---

52 WAYS
To Help Others Win

If this book helps you successfully navigate the challenges of your personal and professional life, I hope you will consider providing a copy for your friends, co-workers or relatives by going to 52waystowin. com.

While you are there please provide some brief comments or recommendations describing any principles or strategies you found especially helpful.

Thanks in advance for helping to empower other leaders!

Tony Ford

book.52waystowin.com

Published by Quirk Ink, an imprint of Quirk Advertising, LLC

To request permissions, contact the team at info@quirkink.com.

ISBN: 978-1-963056-01-3

Cover art and layout by Living Stone Creative, LLC.

Dedication

I dedicate this book to Jane, my wife, best friend, and the love of my life.

Your steadfast encouragement, kindness, and unconditional love have given me the strength and courage to conquer my fears and open my heart!

And to:

My sons—Thanks, Michael and Daniel, you've made being a Dad everything I had hoped for. Your unconditional love, devotion to family, and acceptance have helped me find my way forward in some of life's hardest struggles.

Command Sergeant Major Jack D. Ford—Thanks, Dad, you taught me how to be a good man and a better leader. Your strong, consistent example prepared me to face life with courage.

Larry Ragland—Thanks, Larry, you taught me how to be a Christ-following entrepreneur. You modeled how faith, hope, and love could overcome every obstacle. You are my mentor, my friend, and my example for who I can be in Christ.

I owe all of you more than I can ever repay!

Contents

Foreward   i
Introduction   iv

SECTION ONE: VISION

Preparation   3
Inspiration   7
Vision   13
Perspectives and Expectations   17
Enthusiasm   21
Hope   25
Counting The Cost   29
The Market   35
Stupid Boss, Smart Boss   39

SECTION TWO: LEADERSHIP

Self Motivation   47
Motivating Others   51
Employees   57
Award-Winning P.R.   63
Mentoring   69
Self-Knowledge   73
Reinventing Ourselves   77
Our Mission   81
Exit Strategy   87

SECTION THREE: DISCIPLINE

Focus   95

Choices   99

Balance   103

Opportunities   109

Discernment   113

Tools   117

Transparency   121

Goals   125

Planning or Procrastinating   129

SECTION FOUR: CHALLENGES

Tenacity   137

Courage   141

Distractions   145

Resilience   149

Pain   153

Direction   159

Burnout   165

Struggle   171

SECTION FIVE: CHARACTER

Provision   179

Character   185

Humility   189

Life-Long Learning   193

Gratitude and Stewardship   197

Kindness   201

SECTION SIX: ABUNDANT LIVING

Simple Living   211

Authentic Living   217

Physical Health   223

Marriage   227

Faith   231

Fear   237

Retirement   241

SECTION SEVEN: COMMUNITY

Encouragement   249

Effective Networking   255

Loneliness   263

Celebration   269

Foreward

His License Plate Says, "Love Jane".

It's my privilege to introduce you to a remarkable book authored by my mentor, my business coach, and my friend, Tony Ford. Our journey began over five years ago when I was on the cusp of leaving my full-time job to launch my own business. Tony didn't just become my coach; he became my trusted companion on this exhilarating adventure.

The reason this forward holds such significance for me is simple: it's a tribute to the man whose guidance and wisdom have helped shape my life, my business, and my perspective. I wholeheartedly trust Tony, not just with my career but with my life. He has been a guiding light during my most challenging moments, and I've experienced the transformative power that comes from following his wisdom.

What's truly humbling is that this book could have had a forward from many renowned figures in the business world. But Tony chose me. This decision encapsulates the essence of his philosophy—it's about paying it forward, about nurturing the next generation, and that's why I'm here today.

Tony's experience and wisdom are hard-earned through a lifetime of entrepreneurship. He's started and scaled several successful businesses, each of which addressed market problems—sometimes entirely foreign to him. It's as though he has a sixth sense of business, which has helped him effortlessly navigate the intricate pathways of entrepreneurship.

But Tony's accomplishments extend far beyond profit margins. What sets him apart is his profound understanding of the delicate balance between business and life. He taught me that the bottom line should never eclipse what truly matters—your faith and your family. This principle struck a chord with me, compelling me to stay true to prioritizing my family above all else.

In our recurring meetings, we've celebrated successes and faced setbacks, sometimes with tears but always with unwavering support. It's the sense of camaraderie, the feeling that you're not alone on this journey, that makes Tony's mentorship unique. His introductions have connected me with professionals I wouldn't have met at my stage of growth, propelling my business forward.

Two key lessons have become ingrained in my daily life: First, "If you start it out right, it runs right. If you start it out wrong, you spend the rest of your time trying to fix it." This still sits in the forefront of my mind when I start anything big or small.

The second isn't a quote but a mental image of his license plate that reads "Love Jane." This simple phrase encapsulates his unwavering love for his wife, reminding me to cherish the most important relationships in my life. This is the kind of insight that has the power to reshape your perspective and steer your course toward a richer, more fulfilling life.

As you delve into this book, you'll have the privilege of learning from a man who doesn't just preach wisdom but lives it. The success of the next generation is built upon the foundations laid by those who have walked the path before us, and Tony Ford is one of those pivotal figures in my journey.

His guidance has not only impacted my bottom line but has also taught me the true value of work-life balance. He's demonstrated how to shape our work around our desired lifestyle, not the other way around. These are the insights that have elevated my life beyond business success.

In this book, you'll find quick wins and valuable insights that are tailor-made for the busy professional. Whether you read it cover to cover or extract wisdom from the sections that address your current challenges, it will become an indispensable desk companion, a source of guidance and wisdom as you navigate your own unique path to success.

In closing, Tony, you've taught me how to work smarter, not harder, how to keep faith at the forefront, and how to cherish the connections we make on this journey. Your countless contributions have not gone unnoticed, and I'm committed to paying them forward to others in the future.

Sincerely,

James Thorne

James Thorne is a passionate creator dedicated to empowering individuals, families, and communities through entrepreneurial opportunities. In a career that has spanned a range of industries—from hospitality to ministry, from filmmaking to marketing and business coaching—James has managed teams, led departments, and built several businesses from the ground up. His greatest ambition is to love others like Jesus Christ and to leave behind a legacy of lives changed through financial and spiritual freedom. James is currently the Owner and Chief People Officer for Quirk, Founder and CEO of Vehicle for Good, and Owner of Bow Tie Media. He lives in the heart of Fort Worth with his wife and kids.

Introduction

I have a confession to make.

I am not a fan of most "Business Books". That said, I have read many of them (well, at least the first 50 pages), so I can tell you what seven habits will make you effective, who moved your cheese and where to find it, and which seat on the bus your employees should be in.

My problem with most of these books is that finding the answer to today's problem is just too much work inside of whatever "Schtick" the author has chosen to teach you. Consequently, I have chosen a very different approach in this book. Each of these 52 chapters provides solutions to the real-world issues that almost every leader will deal with if they stick around long enough.

52 Ways To Win is a practical, user-friendly guide to applying your best skills for exploiting opportunities and overcoming obstacles.

I have been an entrepreneur, husband, and father for almost 40 years, and during that time, I have benefitted from the goodwill, generosity, and mentorship of many incredible leaders. As they challenged my ideas and increased my curiosity and capacity for learning, I became convicted that passing on their wisdom was and is my responsibility. So, beginning in 2004, I began writing this book. That's right, it has taken me 19 years to complete what I started and capture the totality of what has been taught to me.

If, at this point you are thinking, "Wow, I'm not sure I want to take advice from a guy that is this slow on the uptake," well, I wouldn't blame you. But consider this: I have had many opportunities to publish this volume. Over the years, I have used these concepts in my own companies, spoken to national audiences, written for business publications, and shared them during my 8,000 hours of coaching entrepreneurs and executives. So why now in 2024?

YOU. I have finally published this book for YOU. Over the last six years of coaching dozens of incredibly aggressive, intelligent young entrepreneurs, I have discovered how effective these ideas and strategies are for them (especially in collaborating with their employees, clients, spouses, and children). I have also become aware of how much harder it is to create a highly productive company and culture in the middle of social media confusion, political instability, financial chaos, and an exploding AI revolution. YOU have it much harder than I ever did while growing my companies.

So, if you are looking for a way to accelerate your personal/professional growth while learning to balance your work and personal freedom— congratulations. I wrote this book for YOU!

To maximize its benefits, start by keeping *52 Ways to Win* close at hand (maybe even on your desk), and when you need a little encouragement or practical direction, go to the chapter that applies.

I will be praying and cheering for your success!

Tony Ford

SECTION ONE

VISION

1

Preparation

If You Start It Out Right—It Will Run Right

Ever wonder why we hate maintenance chores so much?

I believe that our basic disdain for these activities is rooted in the fact that they really do not move us forward; they only allow us not to fall behind. Maintenance is a pervasive reminder that everything around us (including ourselves) is constantly getting dirty, falling apart, or spinning out of control. No wonder substance abuse is at an all-time high!

The chores I love to hate include: taking out the trash, emptying the dishwasher, washing the dogs, folding clothes, washing cars, mowing, weed-eating, and edging the yard (and don't forget "pooper patrol"). Add to this basic personal maintenance: hair, teeth, and nail care, medical, dental, and optical visits, showering, shaving, and sleeping – and on and on it goes.

Understanding how much of our lives are spent, used up, or just plain wasted on trying not to fall behind (much less getting ahead of the Joneses) has become the foundation for my basic life and business philosophy. It goes like this:

"If you start it out right – it will run right. If you start it out wrong – you will spend the rest of your time trying to fix it."

Allow me to explain each part of this concept.

If you start it out right means that future success is almost always dependent on understanding what we are trying to do and how we should go about it. Much of our educational process is based on this premise. That is why securing advanced education greatly enhances career opportunities.

This principle is also true in relationships. Couples who invest time in relationship enrichment classes tend to have more successful marriages with fewer divorces. It is all about the foundation we lay *before* we start building.

In business terms, we sometimes refer to this concept using terms like "due diligence, market research, or pro forma analysis." Fundamentally, *starting out right* means that we gather all of the information we can *before* we commit ourselves and our resources to a course of action.

...it will run right means that success generally follows great preparation. More time invested at the beginning of a project to understand what is needed results in better execution with fewer course corrections and superior outcomes.

The second part of this philosophy is even more instructive and explains a lot about why so many things don't work well:

"*If you start it out wrong*" means relationships, businesses, school projects, or just about anything involving people will go badly in a hurry if we simply choose not to prepare properly. How many times have we said to ourselves, "If I had only known then what I know now?"

In my own life, I find that I "did not know then" because I did not take the time to ask! Ben Franklin was fond of saying that we "Err

in haste and repent in leisure." Speed and efficiency continue to become a higher value in our culture, but that does not diminish the importance of consciously choosing to do things the right way the first time – even if it takes more time. After all, if you don't have time to do it right – when are you going to have time to do it over?
...*you will spend the rest of your time trying to fix it* is indeed the heart of the matter and brings us back to maintenance.

When relationships, projects, or business deals are poorly conceived or researched, future problems are almost *programmed* into them. This is the classic "pay me now or pay me later" scenario.

Success in our personal lives and businesses often depends on how much time and energy we have devoted to the positive aspects of growing and interacting with others. Heading off future problems by investing extra time at the front end leads to a simple and predictable process that yields big returns!

If you start it out right – it will run right.

Growing Forward

Consider taking time this week to strengthen relationships with the important people in your life. Ask the question, "What kind of things are holding back our progress together?" Don't be surprised if you can trace back the answers to something in the past that was set up wrong. Then, make a mutual commitment to go back and set things up right!

Treasure This

"It is not good to have zeal without knowledge, nor to be hasty and miss the way."
Proverbs 19:2, NASB

"It takes as much energy to wish as it does to plan."
Eleanor Roosevelt

"A good plan today is better than a perfect plan tomorrow."
George S. Patton

2

Inspiration

What Makes a Hero

When I was 13 years old, my Dad came home and told us that he had just received orders to go to Vietnam. Even as a boy, I knew that this was very bad news. I knew other kids who had fathers in "Nam", as we called it, and I understood what a scary, difficult struggle it was for them and their families.

Later in the evening, Dad asked me to sit down with him at the kitchen table as he polished his brass and spit-shined his boots. He explained to me that as a Command Sergeant Major with over thirty-one years of active duty (eligible for retirement), he had a choice to make. He could either retire from the Army and pursue a second career or go to Vietnam and become the Command Sergeant Major for the Americal Division. The first choice was safe and sane (and would have made my mom really happy). The second choice was his sworn duty—to defend the United States from all enemies, foreign and domestic. In his mind, it was no choice at all.

Dad explained that a soldier hates war more than anyone because they truly understand the horrific things that happen there. The entire experience is very real and uniquely personal. Yet, knowing this only propels the soldier forward to stand and fight side by side with his comrades. It is a life filled with relationships held together by honor, duty, and interdependence. It is a calling populated with professional people who willingly sacrifice financial rewards and individual recognition for the opportunity to defend their country and fellow citizens. It is a high calling indeed.

As the sun was reflecting low through the backyard window, I noticed that Dad had just screwed the top back onto the Brasso can and that all of his uniform brass was gleaming in the reflected light. I realized for the first time that, unlike my friends, my Dad had never once *ordered* me to shine his brass or his boots. So I asked him about it.

I said, "Dad, how come you have never made me shine your things for you?"

With a surprised look and a curious grin, he said, "Son, someday you will have your own brass and boots to shine. This is *my* brass. These are *my* boots. They are *my* responsibility—not yours."

It was at that moment I understood why heroes are not like the rest of us. Heroes do not see their duty as heroic or as something to be delegated. The very notion of having someone else take their place (in the fight or shining their brass) is totally outside of their way of thinking. For them, it is simple; almost reflexive. To do *my* duty, to honor *my* fellow soldiers, to serve *my* country—it's not just what I signed up for; it is who I am!

A few days passed, and my Dad left for Vietnam. While he was there, he flew over 300 hours in helicopters (crashed three of them), lost several good friends, helped many others come home safe, and returned to us a year later. It was a hard year for him and us. But looking back, we all learned from the experience and would do it again.

A year after his return, my Dad's retirement ceremony was scheduled. By chance, it was set for the same day as my own high school awards ceremony. To me, it was perfect timing. When Dad said that he would try to get the Army to reschedule his ceremony, I said, "*no way!*"

Even though I knew that I was to be recognized with several achievement awards and scholarships at my event, it seemed fitting that I could choose to attend his retirement ceremony instead. It was in this small way that I was able to demonstrate to him just how much I admired his service and his life example to me as a professional soldier.

Dad's retirement ceremony was replete with all of the pomp and circumstance befitting such a hero. The parade field and stands were filled with people of all ages, ranks, and occupations wishing to honor him. Dozens of people, from Sergeants to Generals, surrounded him when it was over to say, "Thanks, Sergeant Major." Many had been raw recruits that he turned into soldiers decades before.

The opportunity to shine my Dad's brass and shoes would finally come years later. After 18 years of retirement, two new careers at the county courthouse, and three grandchildren, Dad did what old soldiers do. He faded away. As we made arrangements to bury him beside the men and women he had served alongside, it came time to prepare his "dress blues" uniform. I polished his medals and buckle to a sparkling luster—just as he liked them.

When the time came to spit-shine his shoes, I polished them with my tears.

Growing Forward

Take some time this week to look around. Chances are that you have heroes in your life that you have not spent much time with lately. Make the time, honor them, and you may learn some valuable things about yourself in the process.

Treasure This

"Greater love has no one than this, that a person will lay down his life for his friends."
John 15:13, NASB

The Gettysburg Address

"Four score and seven years ago our fathers brought forth on this continent a new nation, conceived in liberty, and dedicated to the proposition that all men are created equal. Now we are engaged in a great civil war, testing whether that nation, or any nation so conceived and so dedicated, can long endure. We are met on a great battlefield of that war. We have come to dedicate a portion of that field as a final resting place for those who here gave their lives that that nation might live. It is altogether fitting and proper that we should do this. But in a larger sense we cannot dedicate, we cannot consecrate, we cannot hallow this ground. The brave men, living and dead, who struggled here have consecrated it, far above our poor power to add or detract. The world will little note, nor long remember, what we say here, but it can never forget what they did here. It is for us the living, rather, to be dedicated here to the unfinished work which they who fought here have thus far so nobly advanced. It is rather for us to be here dedicated to the great task remaining before us, that from these honored dead we take increased devotion to that cause for which they gave the last full measure of devotion, that we here highly resolve that these dead shall not have died in vain, that this nation, under God, shall have a new birth of freedom, and that government of the people, by the people, for the people, shall not perish from the earth."

Nov. 19th, 1863

Abraham Lincoln

3

Vision

Standing on the Shoulders of Giants, You Can See a Long Way

Have you ever known a real visionary?

By visionary, I mean a person who seems to know more and see further down the road than the rest of us. Maybe you are one of those people. If so, you may feel that the title sometimes makes you a little uncomfortable. It just seems too big for a regular person to wear somehow.

We often remember visionaries who were great politicians, physicians, scientists, philosophers, or explorers. Names like Benjamin Franklin, Dr. Jonas Salk, Homer (the Greek, not the cartoon character), and Christopher Columbus come to mind. Most probably never realized that they were any different from their peers—they simply were living out who they were and following their curiosity.

One of these people was the seventeenth-century scientist Isaac Newton, who was fond of saying, "We are as dwarfs standing on the shoulders of a giant that we may see even farther than them." Now, as word pictures go, you would have to agree that this is a very descriptive phrase. Not only do we have the juxtaposition of dwarfs and giants, but in using the giants for this purpose, the dwarfs gain a huge advantage. This strikes me as typical entrepreneurial behavior.

Pretty smart guy, this Newton fellow. Unfortunately, while he is often credited with this insightful statement describing the visionary process, it was not his original idea. That honor goes to a man named Bernard of Chartres. Bernard made this statement as part of a book he wrote in 1159 called *Metalogicon*. Even back then, people realized that every visionary relies on the work and understanding of their predecessors to gain insights into the future.

This brings me to my point. If a man as brilliant as Sir Isaac Newton depended on a 400-year-old quote—and 500 years later, we are still quoting him—where exactly is the visionary part of this idea? The answer is profoundly simple and gets to the very heart of what I believe truly defines visionary leadership.

Visionary leaders are people who are gifted at gathering a great quantity of information and then distilling it all down to its most important and relevant essence. They will drain an entire ocean of knowledge in order to dredge up a single perfect pearl of wisdom.

As we seek to manage and grow our businesses, it is important to keep in mind that part of our role as entrepreneurs is to consistently bring our personal vision to the enterprise. When we get too busy to gather the information needed to make informed decisions, our vision becomes dim and ineffective in a hurry. Not only do we become confused and disorganized, but the negative effects ripple through our people and create a culture of anxiety and apprehension.

With this in mind, I encourage you to take advantage of every opportunity that comes your way to stretch your "visionary muscles." As your vision becomes clearer—your company will grow stronger.

You and your people will join the likes of Newton, "standing on the shoulders of giants"!

Growing Forward

Think back to people who have generously shared their time, insights, experiences, and even mistakes to help you grow. Write down the most impactful things they taught you and how those things have helped you navigate your personal and professional life. If possible, reach out to them with a short note of thanks, reminding them of how they blessed you.

Treasure This

"How blessed is the man who finds wisdom, And the man who gains understanding. For its profit is better than the profit of silver, And its gain than fine gold."
Proverbs 3:13-14, NASB

"We can only see a short distance ahead, but we can see plenty there that needs to be done."
Alan Turing

"The wise man must remember that while he is a descendant of the past, he is a parent of the future."
Herbert Spencer

4

Perspectives and Expectations

Seeing What Others See

Allow me to introduce you to my faithful hounds – Samson and Goliath.

Samson and Goliath are four-year-old Golden Labrador Retrievers. They are brothers and could not be more different. Samson is oversized for a Lab, weighing in at just over 105 pounds. He spends most of his time lying around waiting for something to run across our back pasture, at which time he will decide if it is worth chasing. Goliath is a smaller dog (only about 85 pounds) and will chase anything that moves (or blinks, or twitches, or flies – you get the idea). I call him "Young Hyper Dog." Two brothers – two completely different views of the world around them.

Every morning, I start our day together by getting up around 6:00 a.m., grabbing a cup of coffee, and stumbling out to the back porch to give them their morning rations. As the sun is just beginning to kiss the horizon, they eat while I enjoy the sounds of the country and try to wake up. About the time I am ready for my second cup, they have finished eating and are ready for their daily treat—dried pigs' ears. The next 15 minutes are almost always our best time of the day. I am busy writing notes to myself for the chapters I want to write that day while they chew and slobber hungrily on the ears. At this point each morning our expectations for the remainder of the day often conflict.

You see, from my perspective, it is time to go get cleaned up and drive over to my office to put in a hearty day of work. Their expectation is that not only will I stay home with them but that we will all retire to our nice air-conditioned living room for an early morning siesta. This situation is partially my fault because that is our normal drill on Saturday mornings after I mow the yard. Not having the benefit of a calendar, wristwatch, or opposing thumbs somewhat limits their ability to fully comprehend how my normal weekday routine differs from the weekend. And therein lies the rub (and the example).

Not only are they offended by the fact that I am leaving them outside in the heat, but they know that we keep the house nice and cool all day while we are gone. From their perspective, this is a total waste of resources. At a bare minimum, they should be able to take advantage of our wastefulness by being permitted to stay inside. What they are not able to appreciate is the fact that my wife Jane does not enjoy coming home from a hard day's work only to find her nice clean house covered in dog hair. Vacuuming at 7:00 p.m. every weekday night is not on her schedule.

This true but rather silly example of conflicting perspectives and expectations brings us to some important points to keep in mind as we seek to effectively work with our employees, customers, and vendors:

- Most people feel very strongly about their own perspectives and expectations.
- Not every expectation is realistic—but it is very real to the person who has it.
- Perspectives drive expectations and vice versa.
- Discounting the perspectives or expectations of others is the shortest path to creating serious conflict.

- There is usually some valid (experiential, historical, or psychological) basis for the perspective that a person has, so the best we can do is try to understand it.
- The ability to compromise on "style" issues instead of principles will go a long way in bringing order out of conflicting expectations.
- Sometimes, just being allowed to share and explain our perspectives opens the door for dialog and resolution.
- Two or more conflicting perspectives can all be valid. It is our job as leaders to find practical workarounds that will honor those perspectives while building realistic expectations.

Growing Forward

As you prepare for this week, consider how each of your people (and you) reacts to situations where conflicting perspectives and expectations arise. Think through why each person on your team holds the perspective they do. A great tool to help you with this is to have your folks participate in some personality profiling. This is a simple process for gaining insight into how each interacts with the world and the people around them. The more you know about their perspectives and expectations, the better you will lead.

Two popular profiling tools are: "DISC" and "Culture Index."

Treasure This

"Every person's way is right in his own eyes, But the Lord examines the hearts."
Proverbs 21:2, NASB

"The pessimist sees difficulty in every opportunity. The optimist sees the opportunity in every difficulty."
Winston Churchill

"The most pathetic person in the world is someone who has sight, but has no vision."
Helen Keller

5

Enthusiasm

The Sound of Passion and Success

Go time!

After months of planning, the day was finally here – producing my first radio show.

I found myself sitting in the fifth-floor studio control room looking out over downtown Dallas as the engineer prepared the board and handed me the first set of promotional segments. I quickly read through each one and waited while he reviewed his final pre-recording checklist.

Finally, Ed put on his headphones, looked across the control panel, and said, "OK Tony, I know that you are a naturally enthusiastic guy, but for radio, you have to speak way over the top. When you think you are really over-emphasizing every word and phrase, *that* is just when you are starting to bring enough energy to the process. Remember, they can't see you. You have to put everything you are trying to communicate into your words."

Wow, did I have a lot to learn! For the next few minutes, Ed helped me practice my lines and pointed out ways to raise and lower my voice to bring better meaning to the words. Over and over, he told me to smile as I spoke. Finally, he took my script away and said, "Now you're ready to do this."

"Do what?" I asked.

"Speak with the passion you really have for helping entrepreneurs grow their businesses."

Ed was right. This time, when he counted me down, I knew exactly what I wanted to say and how I wanted to say it. He had shown me how to make my enthusiasm come through over the airwaves. As it turns out, creating a great radio show is really hard work.

As Ed continued to coach me, I realized that I sometimes discount how difficult it is to model real enthusiasm in our lives. While we may feel comfortable sharing our ideas and passions with other business owners and managers in person, on the phone, or via email, some situations require a very different approach. What about at home with our families, in church, or in the community? Simply having enthusiasm is not enough; it's important that we keep learning new ways to communicate it as well.

When I was finished recording my spots, I drove back to my home just west of Fort Worth. I was so jazzed by what I had learned that I could hardly sit still. Noticing that the land around our house was looking a little overgrown, I decided that a few hours on my tractor would be the perfect end to this wonderful day.

My tractor is a fully restored 1957 Ford 601 that has a mind and schedule all its own. When I turned the key, and nothing happened, it became instantly apparent that mowing our backlot today was simply not a part of its agenda. Not to be denied, I went to disconnect the battery cables to give it a boost, only to find that the terminal bolts were rusted solid. So, out came the WD-40. I drowned each one in the hope of salvaging my project before darkness fell.

Thirty minutes later, the penetrating lubricant had done its job, and I was able to get the old girl running again. Bumping along across our field for the next several hours, I replayed the day's events and lessons learned in my mind.

Here is what I came up with:

- As entrepreneurs, we often take ourselves and our business so seriously that the real joy and passion for growing it gets locked up inside us. If others can't see that we are having fun, why would they want to associate with us?
- Nobody will ever understand our business like we do—after all, it's our baby! It is our job to educate and motivate others to see it as favorably as we do.
- Employees, customers, and even vendors are continually forming opinions about us as owners and managers and about our company. Realizing that every interaction is an opportunity to reinforce a positive image is critical to gaining their support for our mutual efforts to help it grow.
- The well of emotion from which we draw our enthusiasm has a finite amount of "living water" within it. To live a healthy and balanced life, we must reserve an appropriate amount of this precious resource to share with our family, friends, outside interests, and ourselves.
- Enthusiasm is a two-way street. We must take a proactive interest in the lives and businesses of others if we expect them to reciprocate. Being enthusiastic about the success of others is an open invitation for them to help us reach our goals.

There have been many times in my life when I discovered that my enthusiasm had become like the stubborn bolts on that old tractor—rusted in place. Often, during those times, friends, family members, employees, and even strangers have come into my life and sprayed me down with WD-40 (encouragement) to free up my passions again.

Who do you trust to help you loosen up?

Growing Forward

Being rusted in place is no way to live (remember the Tin Man in *The Wizard of Oz*). If you find yourself there today or in the future, consider some of the lessons I learned and then purpose to *loosen up* and let the world see your passion and enthusiasm again. Go to a trusted friend or family member and ask them to reflect on some of the areas of your life that may need a little lubrication.

Treasure This

"For God has not given us a spirit of fear and timidity, but of power, love, and self-discipline."
2 Timothy 1:7, KJV

"Enthusiasm is the mother of effort, and without it nothing great was ever achieved."
Ralph Waldo Emerson

"Success consists of bounding from failure to failure without loss of enthusiasm."
Winston Churchill

6

Hope

Our Security and Inspiration

The summer of 1980 was one for the history books. Here in Fort Worth, Texas, we had just experienced three months of 100° + days. My personal summer experience consisted of a daily 100-mile commute to Baylor Medical Center - Dallas, ensconced in the luxury of our non-air-conditioned 1969 VW bus.

Having just completed my second year of seminary training, I now embarked on a three-month sojourn as a hospital chaplain serving in the Cardiac Intensive Care Unit. Any semblance of dignity or style that did not sweat away during my battle with Dallas traffic quickly surrendered to the stress and pressure that accompanies very sick patients. At the tender age of 25, I was truly a boy trying (desperately) to do a man's job.

It was not that I had no experience dealing with difficult situations. By now, I had spent several years as a country club manager, a hotel and restaurant consultant, and a general manager for Steak & Ale. I had worked with employees and customers who were tired, drunk, stoned, angry – and sometimes just crazy! But none of these experiences prepared me for what I saw in the CICU. For the first time in my life, I saw real hopelessness firsthand.

The doctors and nurses in the CICU are incredible people who care for patients undergoing open heart surgery or dealing with critical cardiac diseases. The patients are a mixed group of men and women of all ages. Almost all are very sick and very afraid. Many will not leave the hospital alive—and they know it.

It is against this background of fear and anxiety that I met a very special lady. Her name was Emma, and she was a 67-year-old woman with the spirit of a 12-year-old girl. Her face was lined with wrinkles, and her hair was thin and silvery gray. She was a small woman; although I never actually saw her standing up, I would estimate her to be perhaps five feet tall.

I met Emma about halfway through my chaplaincy tour. I knew her for about 30 minutes.

It was a Thursday morning, and I had been summoned to meet a patient just previous to her surgery time. When I walked into the room, Emma's face lit up as she asked me who I was. I told her that I was the chaplain and asked if she would like to visit with me for a while before her surgery. She said that she would like that very much, so I sat down by her bed, and we began a conversation that would change my life.

I asked Emma a few of the standard "chaplain questions," but very soon, it became clear that she had something she wanted to tell me. Here is what she said:

"Tony, today I will be having my sixth surgery in as many years. I have a chronic disease that attacks and destroys my joints. I have had both elbows, both knees and one hip replaced. In a little while, they will replace the other one."

At that exact time, an orderly came into the room and said it was time for Emma to go to have her hip replacement surgery. Much to my surprise, she asked if I would go down the hall with her as they wheeled her to the operating room—so off we went.

Along the way, Emma told me about her grown children and how proud she was of them. She told me that life had given her so much more than she had ever expected or deserved. Then, as we stopped at the door to the OR, she reached out and grabbed my hand, looked straight into my eyes, and said, "Tony, whatever happens here today, just remember that hopelessness is always premature!" Then the door opened, and she was gone.

I never saw Emma again. And I never heard about how her sixth surgery turned out. But for over 30 years, her words of encouragement in the face of certain pain and debilitation have continued to inspire me.

As an entrepreneur, it can be easy to lose hope. Lack of time, resources, energy, and encouragement has a way of wearing us down. Hope seems to be one of the first casualties in this ongoing war of attrition.

As Emma so eloquently pointed out to me, however, hope is a choice we make. It is a well from which we derive our inspiration to move forward through life. Hope is our alternative to giving up on ourselves and giving in to our fears. In the end, we come to understand what Emma learned through a lifetime of pain and struggles:

"Hopelessness is always premature!"

Growing Forward

Take time this week to take stock of your past and present circumstances. Think about what has happened to bring you to this place in your life. Make a list of all the people and provisions that have lessened your struggle and supported you when things got tough. Then, make your Hope List: a list of the people, provisions, opportunities, and dreams that will fuel your hope for a better tomorrow. Going forward, keep your list close to you and refer to it often. Always choose hope.

Treasure This

My hope is built on nothing less than Jesus' blood and righteousness. I dare not trust the sweetest frame, but wholly trust in Jesus' Name. On Christ the solid Rock I stand, all other ground is sinking sand; all other ground is sinking sand.
Edward Mote, circa 1834 (first appeared in Mote's Hymns of Praise, 1836)

"We must accept finite disappointment but never lose infinite hope."
Martin Luther King, Jr.

"Most of the important things in the world have been accomplished by people who have kept on trying when there seemed to be no hope at all."
Dale Carnegie

7

Counting The Cost

Time to Take a Step Back

Due diligence.

Now there is a term that consultants, management professors and venture capitalists love to put out in front of the rest of us. They wax eloquently on and on about the importance of researching our competition, market trends, and internal capacities. But, to us ordinary entrepreneurs who are just trying to keep our companies growing, what does due diligence really mean?

In a phrase, I like to think of due diligence as *counting the cost* of what we are planning to do. My dogs Samson and Goliath recently provided me with the perfect object lesson to illustrate the process.

It was at the end of our morning ritual, the part where I give them each a dog chew. These particular chews are made from dried pigs' ears. Most of the ears are about 4 inches square and kind of thin. Today, I found one that was at least 10 inches square and almost three times heavier than normal. This one had come from a very large pig!

When I offered this monster ear to Samson, his ears laid back, he tucked his tail between his legs, and he started growling and slowly backing away—never taking his eyes off of the offending object in my hand. Picking up on Samson's instinct for flight instead of fight, Goliath quickly jumped back as well. For two dogs who normally wrestle over a good dog chew, I thought that this was a very unusual response.

Apparently, they had performed their own initial due diligence and decided that:

- This ear is just too big to eat without choking to death
- This thing is so thick and heavy, eating it will cost me a broken canine tooth
- The owner of this ear may come back for it, and I don't want to be around when he does – he is big enough to eat both of us!

Since they obviously were not going to eat the ear, I did what I always do—I reminded them of our rule. "You eat what I offer, or you don't eat at all" (someone has to be in charge around here—and it's not going to be the members of my little furry choir).

Next, I placed the loathsome appendage on the patio table and started walking down to my workshop for my morning workout. At this point, the boys would normally race ahead of me to become my "shop dogs" (meaning they sleep, snore, and pass gas on the shop floor while I sweat on the treadmill). On this day, however, they didn't follow me.

When I got to the end of the path, I turned around to see both dogs moving in slow circles around the patio table. After about 30 seconds of stalking the giant ear, Goliath (the more adventurous of the two) put his front paws on the table, grabbed the ear in his teeth, and pitched it over to Samson, who caught it in mid-air. In the same motion, Goliath pushed himself away from the table, vaulted to his new position opposite his brother, and together they began chewing vigorously on that monster ear.

The next few minutes were a blur of hair, teeth, and bits of ear flying off in all directions. To say the least, it was all pretty impressive.

When the feeding frenzy finally ended, both dogs collapsed in the grass, lying on their side, panting like they were both going to have a heart attack.

Rather than continue down to the workshop, I sat down on the sidewalk and pondered what I had just seen. In their own way, Samson and Goliath had acted out the very essence of what good due diligence is all about.

Here's what I mean. In the face of a new challenge, these animals took the steps most of us would do well to walk through when dealing with our own new experiences:

- Approach with caution—They knew they did not fully understand what they saw, smelled, and sensed. Their first response was to back up and evaluate.
- Assess the situation—What they saw told them this was something they had never encountered before. They were not going to take my word that everything was fine. They chose to take a *wait-and-see* approach (as in, "Where is the rest of this pig hiding?").
- Gather the facts—As they circled around, sniffed, watched, and waited, they concluded that this particular ear would not be a serious threat if they attacked it together.
- Consider the options—Knowing the rule that there would not be another opportunity for a treat today, they decided to *go for it*!
- Rally your resources—Relying on their natural instincts and the dozens of times they had hunted together in the past, they chose to pursue the prey in their own practiced manner.
- Execute the plan with vigor—When the time came to take action, there was no hesitation or second thought. They acted swiftly and in unison. They did not stop until the objective was totally under their control.

- Reap the rewards together—When they finally recovered from their little adventure with the ear, they spent the remainder of the day rolling around and chasing each other. No doubt reliving the glory of their recent victory.

While this story and these illustrations may seem a bit strange or silly, please don't miss the point. The process of due diligence has many parts and takes practice and determination to accomplish.

Need a more *human* example? Let's look at a very old and trusted source for our inspiration this time.

There is a story in the Bible about a king who has been offended by the ruler in a neighboring kingdom. One day, he decided that his only option to save face would be to rally his army, charge across the river that separated the kingdoms, and conquer the other king.

A spy for the second king made his master aware of the plan, and that king brought his own army to the river on the day before the planned attack. When the offended king arrived with his army, he looked across the river, counted all the men, horses, and artillery pieces, and realized that he was significantly outnumbered. He sensed an imminent defeat, and rather than charging across the river as he had originally planned, he sent a messenger with a white flag and an offer of peace between the kingdoms.

So, what happened to the first king's plan to attack his neighbor?

In simple terms, the king counted the cost of going to war. He did his due diligence and realized that he did not have the resources to get the job done. Instead, he considered his options and decided maybe he was *not that offended after all!*

Is it time for you to count the cost of your decisions?

Growing Forward

As entrepreneurs, we are faced with decisions every day that require thoughtful consideration. Take time this week to make a list of things you will have to decide on in the coming days and weeks. Schedule some extra time to gather your facts, ponder them, and weigh the potential effectiveness of your responses.

Remember, sometimes it is time to go to war; sometimes we must pursue peace; and sometimes we do neither—it simply is not our fight. Learning and practicing effective due diligence will give you the facts to choose your course wisely.

Treasure This

"Or suppose a king is going to war against another king. He would first sit down and think things through. Can he and his 10,000 soldiers fight against a king with 20,000 soldiers?"
Luke 14:31, NIV

"Never cut a tree down in the wintertime. Never make a negative decision in the low time. Never make your most important decisions when you are in your worst moods. Wait. Be patient. The storm will pass. The spring will come."
Robert H. Schuller

"This grieved me heartily; and now I saw, though too late, the folly of beginning a work before we count the cost, and before we judge rightly of our own strength to go through with it."
Robinson Crusoe

8

The Market

The Final Arbiter of Our Success or Failure

Several years ago, on a family vacation trip to Canada, I saw something that really caught my attention.

We were walking around a small coastal village that borders on the Saint Lawrence Seaway. As we passed the center of town, I looked down into what appeared to be a sunken parking lot. The area was about 100 yards square, but instead of cars, it was filled with all kinds of boats.

There were small sailing and motor boats as well as very large commercial fishing vessels resting on the muddy bottom. Each boat was tethered with thick ropes to concrete bollards that were spaced about 10 feet apart around three sides of the hole. What was astounding was that the hole was almost 40 feet below ground level!

As a lifelong sailboat sailor, I had seen boats in a lot of strange locations, but this place simply did not make sense. Why were all of them down in that hole?

We continued walking through the village and up into the low foothills that surrounded it. Returning in the late afternoon, we once again came upon the sunken boat area – only now it was not sunken at all. In fact, all of the boats were bobbing in the water only a few feet below the edge of the lot.

As we stood staring at the scene in total shock and disbelief, we noticed a man getting off of one of the boats directly in front of us. As he passed by, I called out, "Hey, can I ask you a question?"

The man stopped and said, "Sure – how can I help you?"

I told him what we had seen earlier that day and asked what had happened to make the boats rise that high so quickly.

His surprising response has stuck with me ever since —"Every day at high tide, they open the flood gates and raise that little bridge over there (now we noticed the narrow outlet to the Seaway with the bridge up) to let folks move their boats in and out of the docking area."

I'll have to admit that at that moment, our collective sighs of understanding were overshadowed by a tremendous feeling of stupidity.

As an entrepreneur, I took away two important lessons from that experience:

- **We often only see what we want to see** – When looking down into the hole that early afternoon, I expected to see the basement of a building under construction or a sunken parking lot. It was my expectation that kept my mind closed to other reasonable explanations.

    » As entrepreneurs and leaders, our challenge is to proactively seek out other people's frame of reference to not be limited by our own. Incorporating these insights into our decision-making process not only maximizes our effectiveness; it builds strong bonds with the people who support us.

- **The movements of the marketplace ultimately determine the success or failure of any company** – Much like the tides of the sea, the ebb and flow of something we cannot control are controlling many aspects of business. Certainly, we must do everything possible to prepare our organizations to innovate, strategize, and compete, but the best companies in a declining market can only be successful for so long.

It is also good to remind ourselves that diversification is critical to success in almost every business. Because so much of what drives our industries is based upon technological discoveries, international trade issues, oil prices, fashion trends, etc., keeping one eye on today and the other on tomorrow is critical.

As leaders, we must be asking, "What's now, what's next, and then what?"

Growing Forward

Think back to an experience you have had that really surprised you. Consider how you viewed the information at the time and what you did with it. Make room this week to review your current and future priorities with an eye toward asking: Where is my company and industry going in the future, and what other things should we be getting into?

Treasure This

"The mind of a person plans his way, But the Lord directs his steps."
Proverbs 16:9, NASB

"The marketplace obliges men, whether they will or not, in pursuing their own selfish interests, to connect the general good with their own individual success."
Edmund Burke

"Look at market fluctuations as your friend rather than your enemy; profit from folly rather than participate in it."
Warren Buffett

9

Stupid Boss, Smart Boss

The Choice is Yours

Hi, my name is _____, and I am a stupid boss.

It is at this point in a typical *12-step program* that a person would announce the manifold transgressions he or she has recently committed against their employees, which has perpetuated their addiction as a *stupid boss*. However, since no such intervention program exists (yet), and for the purposes of our exploration, allow me to list some of the attributes that qualify one for this all-too-common job title.

A Stupid Boss:

- Hires intelligent people and then treats them like they are incompetent
- Does not know how to trust his team members
- Only listens to people who are complimentary of his management style and decisions and tunes out any critical feedback
- Surrounds himself with followers and fears other leaders
- Never admits when he is wrong

- Places a high value on loyalty, but never returns it to his people
- Thinks no one notices his mistakes
- Has one set of rules for employees and another for himself
- Uses people and loves things
- Hides problems and shortcomings rather than confronting them
- Thinks he is the smartest person in the room
- Takes credit for his people's accomplishments
- Expects great performance but never models it
- Keeps secrets but betrays confidences
- Hides behind his position rather than taking responsibility
- Leads from the back of the pack – never the front
- Passes the buck and blames everyone but himself

Over the last 40 years of growing companies, I have worked for and with my share of *stupid bosses*. Also, for the record, I, too, have done time in this most unflattering of job descriptions. What I have learned through these experiences is that some bosses want to change, and others don't.

As an entrepreneur or leader, if you fall into the category of not wanting to change and you feel that your management style is just fine as it is, then go forward and good luck (but understand that you are treading on dangerous ground). If however, you know that you are not measuring up to the standard you have set for yourself and your people, here are some constructive ways to move from *stupid boss* to *smart boss* status in a hurry:

A Smart Boss:

- Hires the smartest, most aggressive employees he can find
- Quickly determines their best skills and growing edges
- Learns about them as people; their family situation, hobbies, passions, goals, dreams and fears
- Recognizes that they have *fresh eyes* and can see opportunities and problems that more tenured employees may overlook

- Determines how they see the current business and asks for new ideas
- Finds ways to demonstrate and build trust
- Assigns tasks that will stretch their abilities and force them to learn new skills
- Cross trains them in other job areas to keep them interested and engaged in the growth of the company
- Regularly schedules events that celebrate their ideas and achievements
- Finds ways to reward their contributions
- Speaks to them as professionals with respect
- Creates forums for them to feed back ideas and criticisms
- Provides the tools to do their jobs well
- Passes on emotional and financial credit for their efforts
- Takes responsibility with his superiors for his staff members' mistakes
- Expects loyalty and is fiercely loyal in return
- Becomes personally invested in the health and well-being of his people and their families
- Attends important events involving his people (weddings, funerals, etc) when appropriate
- Trusts them to do the *right thing* and disciplines them appropriately when they don't
- Does not tolerate poor attitudes or gossip
- Sets a high personal standard and leads from the front

Obviously, choosing to build a leadership style that incorporates *smart boss* practices will have a very positive effect on your people and company. However, it is important to recognize that the changes you make to yourself are only part of the process. Your previous habits and behaviors have created certain expectations on the part of your employees that will take some time to change. You can't just show up on Monday morning and introduce the new and improved *smart boss*.

Just as you have built your present culture together with your employees, customers, and vendors, you will have to improve it together. Here are some ways to introduce *smart boss* practices to everyone in a way that they can properly adjust to over time:

- Don't make a grand announcement that you have turned over a new leaf and will no longer be a *stupid boss*
- Do choose one area at a time to work on and then become consistent at modeling your new *smart boss* behavior
- Don't expect everyone to notice the changes right away
- Do remember that you have educated these people to *expect* certain actions and reactions from your past behavior
- Don't try to change too much too soon
- Do start with learning more about each employee. Showing that you want to know them as people is a form of *caring* that helps smooth out other tensions
- Don't try a *one-size-fits-all* approach to leading your team members
- Do focus on the fact that every person is an individual and needs to be treated with individual appreciation for their unique gifts and contributions
- Don't worry about being misunderstood as you implement changes
- Do stay focused on the goal of becoming consistent as you implement new methods and behaviors
- Don't stop trusting your people because they make mistakes or lie to you
- Do use each situation to understand why they are *acting out*— there is a reason
- Don't beat yourself up when you revert back to your *stupid boss* behavior
- Do stay focused on the benefits of practicing *smart boss* habits

If you can't improve for yourself, at least do it for your people!

Growing Forward

As leaders, most of us have habits and management styles that could be considered part of both the *stupid* and *smart boss* categories. Take some time this week to determine which of these attributes best define your leadership practices and choose the smartest areas of improvement for you and your people to work on together.

Treasure This

"Masters, do to your servants that which is just and equal: knowing that you also have a master in heaven."
Colossians 4:1, MEV

"So much of what we call management consists in making it difficult for people to work."
Peter Drucker

"There is only one boss. The customer. And he can fire everybody in the company from the chairman on down, simply by spending his money somewhere else."
Sam Walton

SECTION TWO

LEADERSHIP

10

Self Motivation

It's Not Just About You

The final turn of the final lap of the final race of the season is just up ahead. You choose to go low to maintain the half-second lead you have on Dale Earnhardt Jr., who is sliding up in your slipstream. As you come out of the turn, he makes his move and pulls up right next to your driver's side door. Your eyes meet, and both of you understand that now this race is in the hands of your engine builder. Both machines scream as they top 12,000 RPMs. You flash under the checkered flag as 50,000 NASCAR fans stand cheering.

Then, in a fraction of a heartbeat, you hear the roar of screeching metal as your right front fender evaporates in a torrent of flame and flying debris. Your momentary lack of concentration at the finish line has doomed you and your machine to swift and certain destruction. You close your eyes tight and wait for the final crushing collision – then nothing.

You wait. *Am I dead? Is this Heaven? Or...?*

Finally, as the sweat pours down your forehead, you open your eyes and notice the flashing red lights, the screaming siren, the dark, unnatural shadows.

Once again, it is time to get up and face the day. Your flashing alarm clock will not be denied its power over your life. And what a shame—you almost won the race this time.

Ever find it hard to get up in the morning to face your workday? Ever play hooky just because you are the boss and no one will challenge you about it?

As entrepreneurs, most of us are *self-starters*. That is to say, we are internally motivated by some force that pushes us forward, even though we often do not want to go. So, what is it that motivates us so effectively (even when we are sick or just plain exhausted)?

For some of us, it is the love of money, power, or control. For others, it is the sense of duty or responsibility. Still others simply have a genuine love for the activities required to be the boss.

If we are honest with ourselves, we may discover that on any given day, our motivations for coming to work and doing our jobs change. In order to lead effectively, it is important that we pay close attention to these motivations and understand how our attitudes and actions are being observed by our people.

Each time a leader walks into their place of business, the atmosphere instantly changes. Employees intuitively determine whether the boss is happy, sad, angry, tired, disorganized, or stressed. They then internalize these understandings and decide how they should act and interact around him or her.

If the boss is tired and angry, the employees take it as informal permission to complain and blame others for problems. If the boss is happy, the employees feel a sense of security and optimism. This cause and effect takes place over and over as the day goes on.

The fact that the leader's internal state often translates into the attitudes and behaviors of their subordinates is critical to the success of the company—both positively and negatively. This brings us back to the issue of self-motivation.

Because most leaders are internally motivated and because *leaders hire in their own image*, there is often an expectation that everyone is self-motivated. If this were true, however, everyone would be leading their own company. The fact is, most people are followers and depend on the verbal and non-verbal signals they get from their leaders to get and stay motivated. This reality puts a very heavy burden of performance on many entrepreneurs.

So, as leaders, bosses, and entrepreneurs, we have a choice to make every morning and throughout the day. Will we reach inside our own hearts and minds to capture and hold out our vision for the folks around us to see, or will we give in to our own desire for satisfaction and security and simply act as we please?

The mantle of leader is not for everyone. But thankfully, it is seldom bestowed on people who don't somehow seek after it. When we come to the place where our responsibilities overwhelm our abilities, it is time to reach out for help. It is much better to admit that we are maxed out than to drag others into our personal collision and destruction. Sometimes, leadership is about choosing not to lead at all. Each of us has to decide what our limits are and work to stay within a healthy reach of them.

Remember that the goal of self-motivation is to compete vigorously and finish the race strong!

Growing Forward

Take some time this week to think about what things are driving you right now. Make a list of them. Then, sort the list into what is healthy and constructive and what is damaging and destructive. Build your life and company on the healthy parts, and your employees will become your greatest fans as you move into the victory lane together.

Treasure This

"For though the righteous fall seven times, they rise again, but the wicked stumble when calamity strikes."
Proverbs 24:16, NIV

"Success is not final, failure is not fatal: it is the courage to continue that counts."
Winston Churchill

"Keep away from small people who try to belittle your ambitions. Small people always do that, but the really great ones make you feel that you, too, can become great."
Mark Twain

11

Motivating Others

What People Really Want

Thousands of books and articles have been written on the subject of motivation. Consequently, it would be silly for me to presume that I can properly deal with this subject in just a few paragraphs. However, I believe there is a subtle truth about how we motivate others that every entrepreneur must understand to be effective.

The first part of this truth is most companies motivate people by *fear of loss* rather than by *hope of gain*. You can confirm this opinion for yourself by simply watching TV or picking up a magazine. Pay attention to the basic premise of each advertisement:

Car ads:
- "Hey guys! Drive a flashy car because women love that." *Real message: no flashy car = no beautiful ladies in your life.*
- "Hey guys! Our truck can tow an entire house. Don't get caught driving a wimpy truck." *Real message: no 4-wheel drive monster truck = no bragging rights.*

Cosmetic ads:

- "Attention ladies! Our perfume, make-up, and lotions will make you uber attractive to handsome, cultured men." *Real message: no high-end cosmetics on your bathroom counter = no upwardly mobile dates in your future.*

- "Tired of lipstick that only lasts a few hours? Ours lasts for days and will make you really stand out from all the other women." *Real message: wear another brand of lipstick, and you will get lost in the crowd.*

I picked these two product offerings because they are so stereotypical of the way Madison Avenue magnifies our deficiencies in order to create demand for their products. This kind of negative *fear of loss* motivation has become the normal methodology for promoting most products and services.

The multiplied effect of these messages over many decades has given people a type of universal inferiority complex. As my wife often reminds me, "The reason models are called models is because *they are not a normal part of the population*—they (not we) are the anomaly. Normal folks just aren't blow-dried and made up with perfect teeth and skin." Just try to find all these pretty people the next time you are on a cruise ship.

The second part of this truth is actually very good news for enlightened entrepreneurs. Because we understand that most advertising contains a *fear of loss* message, we can position our processes and offerings to counter that embedded negativity. Our company can become a *positive alternative.* This elevates what we say and do to a position of hope and optimism as opposed to fear and dread.

Here are some ways we can positively demonstrate this to our customers, employees, and vendors:

Customers:

- Create a *Customer Counsel*—Several times each year, bring a group of customers to your facility or a nice hotel and solicit their input on how you can provide them with better products and services. Make it all about them and their needs. Create an atmosphere of openness and resist the temptation to push your needs or make excuses. Follow up by providing them with the kinds of products and solutions they asked for. Commit to doing this every year.

- Treat them as equals—Even if your company is much larger or provides exclusive access to certain products or services, proactively treat even the smallest customer as a peer. Remember that customers talk to each other and that the ones who are small today may someday be your largest source of revenue. Respect everyone.

Employees:

- Stay close to them—Create regular opportunities for your employees to interact with senior managers and owners. Our companies have bi-weekly "brown bag lunches" where all company employees are invited to spend 90 minutes having lunch with the owners. They give us advice on what is and is not working, and we take pages of notes. The notes become part of our focus to move the company forward. Everyone wants to be heard—especially by the boss.

- Celebrate, Celebrate, Celebrate—People motivate themselves more by gaining a little recognition than by any number of raises they receive. Recognize birthdays, anniversaries of years served, outstanding performances, etc. Remember to make these recognitions company-wide. It is easy to forget the folks in administration or the warehouse—don't wait till they walk off the job in frustration to recognize them!

Vendors:

- Proactively praise them—Go out of your way to give your vendors and their representatives positive feedback whenever possible. Just as you and your employees have a job to do, their job is to serve you and your competitors. When the time comes that the products you need from them are in short supply or you have to wait a few extra days to pay their invoices (and you will), the small investment you have made by encouraging them will pay big dividends.

Motivating others is about giving them what they really want. Short-term manipulation using thinly veiled negative messages may give us immediate results, but healthy companies and lasting relationships depend on creating mutual respect and positive interactions.

You're the boss—proper motivation starts with you!

Growing Forward

Take some time this week to consider some of the actions mentioned in this chapter and decide which ones you are willing to try. It may be that you discover a whole new way to motivate and energize your people.

Treasure This

"And let's consider how to encourage one another in love and good deeds, not abandoning our own meeting together, as is the habit of some people, but encouraging one another; and all the more as you see the day drawing near."
Hebrews 10:24-25, NASB

"People underestimate their capacity for change. There is never a right time to do a difficult thing. A leader's job is to help people have a vision of their potential."
John Porter

"Twenty years from now, you will be more disappointed by the things that you didn't do than by the ones you did do. So throw off the bowlines. Sail away from the safe harbor. Catch the trade winds in your sails. Explore. Dream. Discover."
Mark Twain

12

Employees

<hr />

Making Them *Your* People

The phone rings at 1:00 on Sunday afternoon just as you are about to lie down on your favorite napping chair. The voice on the other end is your National Sales Manager calling from the county jail. He wants to know if you will come down and bail him out.

You sit down to dinner with your wife. It's Friday night and the end of another long week of trying to solve customer problems with one hand and increase sales with the other. Finally. *Finally*, you get time with just the two of you—alone. Your cell phone rings, and it is one of your warehouse workers calling to tell you that his mom has just passed away.

The traffic is light, the weather is great and you have just put down your briefcase ready to work through all of the "to-dos" that are still waiting to become "the dones." Your assistant walks in and says, "I just talked to Betty in the sales department. Her daughter Julie just got hit by a car as she was walking to school this morning—the ambulance is taking her to the hospital downtown."

Now, as the company owner, what do you do?

Many owners simply take a *hands-off* attitude when it comes to things that happen to their employees away from the workplace. The thinking here is either, "It is none of my business as an owner" or "There are just too many of them for me to take anything other than a professional interest in." After all, if I get involved in their personal problems, when will I have any time for my own family?

Other owners (especially those with limited outside relationships) find themselves becoming personal friends with many of their employees. They know all of the problems and issues each person is dealing with in their private lives and focus a lot of time and energy on trying to resolve non-work related situations.

In my opinion, both of these approaches hold the potential for creating real problems within the organization and between the owner and the employees.

Completely isolating ourselves from the personal issues of our employees causes them to adopt a "them vs. us" mentality that spills over into their work performance and attitudes. It also works against our ability to build a culture of trust and mutual support. Company owners that adopt this model tend to have high turnover, increased theft, low job satisfaction, and poor productivity.

Owners who become too involved in the private lives of their employees create an unhealthy environment as well. Here, the high value becomes friendship rather than the productivity and the goals of the company. These owners quickly become conflicted in their ability to supervise and fairly appraise the performance of their employees. Companies that get caught up in this scenario find themselves slow to react to market opportunities because the leader is so distracted.

I selected each of the three scenarios outlined at the beginning of this piece from literally dozens of situations involving my own employees over the last 40 years. You can add to these a variety of routine situations like finding someone who is drunk, high, or asleep on the job, steals, lies, or sleeps with many of their fellow employees. Consequently, it doesn't take long for even the most enlightened leader to feel like washing their hands of the whole mess.

In our companies, we have adopted several guiding principles designed to demonstrate our personal commitment to our people while maintaining firm boundaries that everyone is expected to respect. Here are some of them:

- When an employee or a member of their immediate family is in the hospital, one of the owners visits at least once.
- When an employee or a member of their immediate family is having surgery or a baby, one of the owners sits with the employee.
- When an employee is in an abusive situation and wants out, we assist in facilitating the process in cooperation with our local mental health and police resources.
- When an employee has an unusual financial need, we provide short-term loans with payments coming out of their next two to six paychecks.
- If an employee wishes to try one of our products, we sell it to them at cost, or if it is under $10, we gift it to them.
- When an employee wants to discuss a private issue, we set a time that day, and one of the owners makes themselves available.

We work hard not to make a big deal about how we handle these situations. Our goal is to keep private matters private. Being proactively involved in supporting our people during these very stressful times has created a culture of mutual respect and caring about others. The greatest compliment we have received as owners has been when we have seen our managers follow our examples of hospital visits and take the initiative to help support their people.

In our company culture it is very important that our folks understand we are here to help them reach their full potential as employees and as people. Many of them never had anyone to model a supportive, tough-love kind of environment. We see that as part of our job as company owners. That's how they become *our* people.

We work hard, we play hard, and we never forget to care hard.

Growing Forward

If any of the principles outlined in this chapter have resonated with you, now would be a good time to discuss them with the senior managers in your company. Most will only work if everyone in leadership buys into them. My advice is to start slow and implement one or two new practices at a time until everyone gets used to interacting with your employees on a more engaged level.

Treasure This

"For I was hungry and you gave me something to eat. I was thirsty and you gave me something to drink. I was a stranger and you invited me in. I needed clothes and you clothed me. I was sick and you looked after me. I was in prison and you came to visit me. I tell you the truth; whatever you did for one of the least of these brothers of mine, you did for me."
Matthew 25:35-36, 40, NASB

"It is one of the most beautiful compensations of life; that no man can sincerely try to help another without helping himself."
Ralph Waldo Emerson

"If you will think about what you ought to do for other people, your character will take care of itself. Character is a by-product, and any man who devotes himself to its cultivation in his own case will become a selfish prig."
Woodrow Wilson

13

Award-Winning P.R.

It's Your Story to Tell

I did not even hear them call my name. All I knew was that an entire auditorium full of very well-dressed people were staring at me all of a sudden. The next thing I knew, I was standing on the stage thanking them and the 60 incredible people who worked with me every day to make the Fort Worth Business Assistance Center a national success.

The occasion for this surreal scene was the 1995 Ernst & Young Entrepreneur of the Year Awards ceremony in Dallas, Texas. As the Executive Director of the FWBAC, I had been nominated for this award in the newly created category of *Supporter of Entrepreneurship*. Several other outstanding organizations were competing for this honor, and since we were the newest among them, I thought our chances of winning were very small. That is why I was in such shock and surprise when the Master of Ceremonies called my name.

As it turns out, this was to be only the first of many awards that the FWBAC would receive. Soon thereafter, it would also be recognized by the President of the United States as a national model for equipping entrepreneurs. All of these accolades were for an organization that had a public relations budget of zero dollars.

I share this experience with you because figuring out how to tell the world about our organization on a small budget seems to be at the top of every entrepreneur's wish list. Since I had already participated in four small company start-ups before implementing the FWBAC concept, working with no marketing funds was second nature to me. What I knew about *marketing on a shoestring budget* from those start-ups was this:

- Build a great story—If you can't explain why your company and its services are different and better, no one else will care about it. Choose two or three things that make your company stand out and then build a compelling story around them.

- Partner in success—Make a short list of who will benefit as you succeed. This should include your employees, vendors, bankers, your customers and their friends, and your building neighbors (if you are in retail, more foot traffic helps everyone). The more these folks like you, your people, and what you all do for them, the more they will help tell your story and bring in new customers.

- Give credit to others—Always brag about everyone in the list above. The more goodwill you show to them, the more motivated they will be to promote your business.

- Lead a happy company—Folks naturally gravitate toward happy people. Go out of your way to keep things fun and positive at your company. Resist the urge to complain about things that are not working well. It is your job to be a fun and positive influence everywhere you go.

- Help others share your story—Get used to the idea that *you have to do the work for them*. Provide potential purveyors of your story with everything they need to tell it correctly. Send short articles about positive employee and customer interactions to social media outlets. Invite local business writers to see how you run your business and to meet your happy employees.

- Give back and get involved—Choose at least two community groups to be actively involved in. Then, find ways to sponsor events using the products or services that your company provides. This is one of the most cost-effective ways to create a positive public image for your organization in a short amount of time. Don't forget to take your own pictures and videos of these events to send to enhance your online presence.

Along with all of these activities, never miss an opportunity to honor your employees, vendors, or company by nominating them for an award.

Internal P.R. – Promote employee high achievement by providing consistent recognition. This can take the form of weekly, monthly, quarterly, and annual performance awards, including gift certificates to local restaurants, stores, movies, and special events. Money can also be the prize, but it is much more meaningful when coupled with a plaque or other trophy item that celebrates the achievement. Even better is to have a floating award like "Sales Rep. of the Month" or "Administrator of the Quarter" that moves from one recipient's desk to another when they win it. Don't underestimate the power of bragging rights amongst your employees.

External P.R. - The opportunity to position your business as an award-winning company is available from a variety of sources. Here are just a few:

Small Business Administration

The SBA has several annual award and recognition programs including: Small Business Person of the Year, SBA Exporter of the Year, Woman Owned Business of the Year, and Small Business of the Year.
(www.sba.gov)

Local Chambers of Commerce

Almost every Chamber of Commerce holds annual competitions

for Business of the Year awards in a variety of categories.
(www.uschamber.com)

Local Business Publications
Most major cities have at least one business magazine/online
publication. Often these magazines hold business plan
competitions, 40 under 40 Awards, or Business of the Year
Awards in a variety of industry categories.

Ernst & Young Entrepreneur of the Year Award
This program started in 1987 and is recognized as the pinnacle
of entrepreneurial achievement. In the last 35 years, more than
15,000 outstanding entrepreneurs have been recognized for
their vision, innovation, courage, and leadership in building
and growing successful businesses. Each year, the new winners
become lifetime members of the Entrepreneur of the Year Hall
of Fame in New York City. (www.ey.com/global/content.nsf/
US/EGCS)

The Malcolm Baldridge National Quality Award
This award program started in 1987 when congress created it
to honor U.S. companies that exhibit a "best of class" standard
of excellence in their manufacturing processes. This award
process sparked the *era of benchmarking*. Attaining this award
requires a company to go through a rigorous battery of process
improvement benchmarking activities that culminate in being
evaluated by a panel of Malcolm Baldridge-certified judges.
The Malcolm Baldridge process has created an entire industry
dedicated to helping make U.S. companies more globally
competitive. (www.quality.nist.gov)

While these awards are some of the most coveted and widely known,
keep in mind that there are literally hundreds of award programs
for which companies can apply. Most only require that you submit
a completed application form and a few references. Also, remember

that if you don't win this year, you can always reapply next year. Tenacity really pays off when it comes to winning these awards.

Once your business has won an award, be sure to mention it on every application you make to other award programs. Generally, award judges want to recognize companies that have an established track record of high achievement. Mentioning previous awards helps them to associate your company with excellent performance and gives you an edge.

Leveraging the awards process to bring recognition to your company and its people is a cost-effective way to get noticed in the marketplace. Not only does your company gain free publicity, an objective third party also validates it. Train your employees (especially your salesforce) to use these awards to separate your business from the pack as they interact with potential customers.

Remember—it's your story to tell!

Growing Forward

As business leaders and entrepreneurs, we are proud of our company, our people, and the work we do together. Since we work so hard to get it right every day, it just makes sense that we should work equally as hard to get our story out. Take time this week to consider how you can use the awards process to gain valuable recognition for your company and your people. Then start applying!

Treasure This

"Neither do people light a lamp and put it under a bowl. Instead they put it on its stand, and it gives light to everyone in the house."
Matthew 5:15, NIV

"Without promotion, something terrible happens... nothing!"
P.T. Barnum

"Any small business that's predicated on technological innovation and is differentiated and superior can expand globally very effectively using the Internet as a vehicle for promotion."
John Quelh

14

Mentoring

Making the Wheel Go Round

Young Squirrel, Professional Second Banana, Go-To-Guy, Main-Man, Second-In-Command, Vice President in Charge of *Everything* the boss does not want to do today—these are just a few of the ways my leaders and mentors have referred to me over the years.

From the time I was very young, I have received the devoted instruction of a variety of incredible people, starting with my Dad, who taught me my earliest lessons about trust, duty, honor, love of country, and integrity. Each one left their own unique impressions on my mind and spirit. All passed on a very precious part of themselves, preparing me to ultimately invest their wisdom in others down the line.

It is this "pay it forward" mentality that is at the very heart of the mentoring dynamic. Simply put, each of us has unique and wonderful knowledge that, left unshared, will come to nothing and profit no one. When we take that knowledge, add a dose of experience, a pinch of insight, and a heaping helping of wisdom, it magically transforms into a recipe for someone else's success. What a gift. What a legacy to pass on!

In my life, I have been blessed to mentor young entrepreneurs one-on-one and work with newlywed married couples along with my wife, Jane. Of the over 200 couples we have discipled during the last 40 years, only one marriage has ended in divorce. This is a powerful example of how effectively mentoring can equip people to overcome the difficulties we all face in our lives.

For those of us who have chosen to live a mentoring lifestyle, the returns on our investment are both surprising and extraordinary. Not only do we develop rich relationships with our students, but we also find ourselves regularly reflecting on how the lessons we teach are being lived out in our own lives. Becoming a great mentor is a rather long and introspective process. Over time, it gets harder and harder to live a "do as I say, not as I do" kind of lifestyle. The mentoring process often propels us to change how we live our lives as much as (or more than) those we are teaching.

The ultimate benefits of the mentoring experience come when a person is both being mentored by someone who has gone down life's road ahead of them and pouring themselves into a younger, less experienced person.

If you have ever considered entering into a mentoring relationship, here are some of the benefits you can expect:

- Your worldview will change dramatically—If two heads are better than one, just imagine how much more you will learn from another person who is totally committed to your success.

- Your understanding of self will improve—Some say that "only people who love us or hate us will tell us the truth about ourselves." A good mentor will care enough to reflect back the truth about areas where personal growth is needed.

- You will learn how to tell the truth—The first thing one of my mentors told me was that it is almost impossible for a young man to tell the truth. He was right. Over the next few years, he helped me gain confidence and learn how to be honest with myself and others.

- You won't be alone anymore—Imagine having a person in your life who really knows you just as you are and wants nothing more than to help you succeed in life. He or she becomes your trusted teacher and main cheerleader.

- You won't take yourself so seriously—Having someone else to share our ideas, fears, hopes, failures, and goals is very freeing. As you become more at ease with yourself, you will be better equipped to productively interact with other people.

- You won't have to fail before you succeed as much—If you really pay attention, your mentor will be able to warn you about attitudes, activities, and opportunities that are really just unforeseen traps. Your job is to listen, trust, and learn from their past mistakes. Developing this skill will put you years ahead of your peers.

- You will become hungry to pass on what you have learned— Mentoring is an infectious process. One day, someone will walk into your life, and you will say to yourself, "I think that I could really help that person grow." Then, you will have to step outside of your comfort zone and become a mentor yourself.

As an Army Brat, I spent the early years of my life growing up overseas and in cultures where mentoring and apprenticeship have been an accepted way of life for thousands of years. So naturally, I find it ironic that we as a society are just now coming to understand the profound nature of the mentoring experience. But hey, better late than never.

Now that we in the Western world are becoming aware of the multiple benefits of mentoring, I hope we will continue making it *our* new way of life.

This is your time to find a mentor and become a mentor!

Growing Forward

I challenge you to look around for someone you respect and would like to learn from. Have a conversation with them about the possibility of entering into a mentoring relationship. Don't be surprised if they tell you they have been thinking the same thing – bright people attract each other!

Treasure This

"Go therefore and make disciples of all the nations, baptizing them in the name of the Father and the Son and the Holy Spirit, teaching them to observe all that I commanded you; and lo, I am with you always, even to the end of the age."
The Great Commission, Matthew 28:19-20, NASB

"Mentor: Someone whose hindsight can become your foresight."
Author Unknown

"Mentoring is a brain to pick, an ear to listen, and a push in the right direction."
John Crosby

15

Self-Knowledge

Trading Blind Spots for a Bright Future

The setting: a filthy desert military outpost in North Africa, circa 1943. In one of the first scenes from the movie *Patton*, the general has just assumed command of a poorly disciplined tank division and is conducting his first inspection tour of the facilities and its soldiers.

As he walks around a corner in a barracks building, he trips over the sleeping body of a weary and out-of-uniform soldier. The soldier jumps to his feet, ready to confront the man who so unkindly awakened him. When he sees it is a three-star general, he quickly comes to attention and posits a pathetic salute. Then Patton asks, "What are you doing down there on the floor, soldier?"

The private replies, "I was trying to get some sleep, sir!" To which Patton responds, "Well, get back down there—you're the only S.O.B. in this outfit that seems to know what the hell he is trying to do!"

This entire scene flashed through my mind one morning as I was stuck in heavy Dallas traffic. An old pick-up truck in front of me had a hand-painted sign in the rear window that said: *LOW BID*

PLUMBERS, INC. Reading the sign and remembering the scene from Patton, I thought, "Well, at least someone out here knows what it is he is trying to do." And it wasn't me. You see, I was on my way to another meeting that felt meaningless, that would ultimately fail to move me toward my real goals and desires. I was just going through the motions.

All of that to say, sometimes we find ourselves out of touch with who we are (or are becoming) and what it is we are supposed to be doing. Often, we allow circumstances, opportunities, and other people's agendas to dictate how we live our lives.

As entrepreneurs, we tend to think that just because we are positively brilliant at some things, we must be pretty good at most things. It is this unrealistic belief that so often takes us away from focusing on using our best skills. Like the dog that runs after the school bus every time it passes by, we have no conscious idea of why we are doing what we are doing.

Self-knowledge is about knowing who we are, what we are passionate about, and what we are gifted in—and then committing to finding work that fulfills all of these components. It is the opposite of a mindless pursuit. It is very purposeful and consistently focused. It is hard, grown-up work.

The basic difficulty in attaining self-awareness may explain why bookstore "How To" sections are overflowing with volumes on the subject. Based on the time and ink dedicated to correcting our deficiencies, we have to believe self-ignorance must be some kind of global epidemic. However, I don't believe that learning to understand ourselves has to be that difficult.

I try to do at least three things each day to make myself more aware of how my life is working out:

- Stay close to my family and friends —Only the people who love you will take the time to keep you on the right path in life.

- Stay firm in my faith—God knows my heart and my intentions. He also knows my limitations and can bring people and circumstances into my life to make the most of both.

- Keep asking, "What's next?"—Life is not over until it's over. As long as I am in this world, there are things I can do to contribute. But choosing the right things to do with my time is up to me.

A leader's first responsibility to his or her people is to be self-aware and to work from their best skills. The natural outcome of honoring these priorities will be to grow a healthy organization that allows each person to work out of their own giftedness.

Your organization will only rise as high as its leadership!

Growing Forward

Take some time this week to think back on the last time you really felt at peace with who you are and where your life is headed. If it was recently, and you know you are still on the right track, great! If not, consider getting a helping hand from a trusted friend, pastor, mentor, close relative, or hired expert to reconfirm your passion and purpose in life.

Treasure This

"The second is this: 'You shall love your neighbor as yourself.' There is no other commandment greater than these."
Mark 12:31, NASB

"It is the greatest good for an individual to discuss virtue every day...for the unexamined life is not worth living."
Socrates

"We don't see things as they are; we see them as we are."
Anais Nin

16

Reinventing Ourselves

Becoming a Better *You*

In about two hours, my wife and I will sign the contracts that will finalize the sale of our company to one of our largest competitors. After 14 wonderful years, it is finally time to give up the fight and join forces. For Jane, it will mean a brief transition time with the combined company, then the start of her next career. For me, it means I have to leave the building—forever. Nothing personal, but most purchasing companies don't want the former CEO hanging around any longer than it takes the ink to dry!

Since we have been planning this transition for many months, the idea of moving on is not new for me. Also, having participated in the formation and transition of several other organizations in the past, like Yogi Berra said—"it seems like deja vu all over again." Having said that, moving on from this particular company is harder for me than the others have been for several reasons.

First, I have had the privilege to build Salon Support, Inc. working side by side with Jane. I have seen her blossom from a very accomplished corporate business analyst (17 years with IBM) into a gifted operating officer and entrepreneur. She is a natural leader that people automatically warm to and trust.

Second, I really enjoyed working with the high caliber of people we were able to attract as a dominant force in our industry segment. We had a low turnover, and many of our employees practically grew up with us. I know their folks and their kids. I will miss them a lot.

Third, my new career as a writer and speaker is something a bit foreign to me. It brings with it a strange mixture of excitement and terror—as it should. In my humble opinion, people who do not have a healthy fear of the unknown are simply not paying attention!

If the old saying "practice makes perfect" applies to the personal reinvention process, I should be within spitting distance of perfection any time now. Since I know that I am not, I have to believe that I am either doing something fundamentally wrong, or this process just cannot be mastered. In a meager attempt to salvage my bruised ego in all this, I choose to vote for the second option.

Given then that personal reinvention really may be a unique and elusive process, the best way I can help you understand is to share some common lessons that I have learned in 40 years of taking on new careers.

As you contemplate making a major change of direction—whether in your business or personal life—look for these signposts to help you along the way:

- Be yourself—Reinventing ourselves is a waste of time if we settle for becoming someone we are not. Business partners, employees, vendors, friends, and even family members often push us to act and be someone we were not meant to be. Decide who you really are, and then go surround yourself with work and play that will feed into the real you.

- Don't look back—I have read countless resumes that state, "Ten years of experience …" When I ask the candidate about recent accomplishments and learning, it often mirrors what they did in their initial years. In reality, they've repeated two years of experience five times. Looking back can lead us to replay past experiences and habits. Now is the time to look forward and try new things.

- Don't settle – Sometimes, when we reach forward to try new and different things, the money runs out before the opportunity fully matures. My advice is: don't settle. It is better to sell your big house and "stuff" in order to gain a new and fulfilling life than to find a job doing what you have always done – just to pay the bills.

- Work hard—Nothing worth having comes easy. Now is the time to get your mind right about the struggles and obstacles that lie ahead. It is also a good idea to get the buy-in of your spouse and close friends. Things will be kind of messed up for a while, but it won't be that way forever. With hard work and focus, you will find your way and your new normal.

- Have fun—Reinventing ourselves is not worth much if we don't enjoy the process and learn to laugh at ourselves from time to time. Hey, this is new territory! Of course you are going to take some significant detours and get lost along the way. Get used to it; there are lessons to be learned in the journey, and lots of them!

- Don't sweat the small stuff—Just like making sausage, reinventing ourselves is not always pretty to look at. Keep your eyes on the end goal—a new start for a new you and doing work that makes you feel great. Learn to let go of things that don't move you forward. With a little practice, you will become an expert on what is and is not important to the process.

The future is a big place filled with
opportunities and obstacles
—now is the time to get ready!

Growing Forward

Let's face it: you may have never even thought about "reinventing yourself." Take some time this week to really consider if your life is what you had hoped it would be. If it is, great! If it is not, now may be a good time to start thinking about the new you. Go for it.

Treasure This

"And do not be conformed to this world, but be transformed by the renewing of your mind, so that you may prove what the will of God is, that which is good and acceptable and perfect."
Romans 12:2, NASB

"The reinvention of daily life means marching off the edge of our maps."
Bob Black

"I think reinvention for all of us is not a nice-to-do; it's a got-to-do."
Carly Fiorina

17

Our Mission

Faithfulness Costs and Rewards

1967

The Six Day War between Egypt and Israel had just begun.

Vietnam had become a mess for the U.S.

American politics was now a contact sport attracting radicals and protesters nationwide.

The Cold War was heating up as Russian tanks rolled into Poland.

I was lying in a British Army hospital bed in Muenster, Germany, having undergone emergency surgery to repair a hole in my large intestine. Only a few hours earlier, I had almost bled to death when my diverticulum burst as I was playing soccer with my friends.

Now, I awoke to find myself surrounded by a scruffy, smelly group of very large, very tough-looking men. I closed my eyes and drifted back into a restless unconsciousness. This 12-year-old American boy was having a very strange dream!

A few hours later, I awoke to find that I had been relocated to a barracks-like ward occupied by four other beds. After passing in and out of sleep for the next several hours, I finally became fully awake to realize that this was no dream. Presently, there were four young soldiers standing over my bed.

"Who are you guys?" I asked.

With a deep laugh and a grin that revealed several missing teeth, one of the burlier among them replied, "We are Her Majesty's tank soldiers—Tankers for short)—and we have been ordered to watch over you until you heal up. *You are our new mission!*"

As I looked closely at these men, I realized, like me, each was recovering from some kind of surgery or injury.

Jerry, the red-haired, freckle-faced comedian of the group, had lost two fingers when his tank's turret lopped them off in a training accident.
Frank, the skinny, quiet one, had broken his arm and ankle falling into a mortar crater during a night mission.

Jimmy hobbled around my bed with his crutches and leg cast, looking very serious. But his dour expression melted away when he told stories about growing up as a lad in Ireland.

Best of all, there was Pete. He was an affable Londoner with bright green eyes, ears that were far too large for anyone's head, and a love for adventure books that would soon infect me. Like Jimmy, Pete's leg was broken and in a cast.

For the next five days, this small band of brothers hovered around me like a group of worried daddy penguins warming an egg. Looking after me and my needs was their mission, and they took it seriously. I learned a lot from each of these men, but it was Pete and his love for reading that influenced me the most.

Each of the men took shifts looking after me, but Pete would often volunteer to sit in for some of the others, especially late at night. I knew that the cast on his leg started to hurt after sitting in one place for a while, but he would insist on remaining by my side, hour after hour, reading and talking to me.

On the second day we were together, Pete asked me if I liked adventure books. I said that I did not read much except for school books. I told him I never had much time for it, with sports and everything. He then opened an old leather satchel and took out a ratty, dog-eared copy of *Treasure Island*. For the next two hours, the soldier read the book to me. From the excitement in his voice and the anticipation that came with each turn of a new page, it was obvious this story was one of his personal favorites.

As the days and nights passed and I became stronger, we were trading off who would read to whom.

Looking back, it is amazing to me that in spite of their own pain and discomfort, young soldiers like Pete chose to invest so much time and effort in helping me learn to love reading. They took their duty seriously; each man became totally committed to the mission he was given. This band of brother-soldiers would never know how many lives they changed because they chose to go above and beyond their orders in taking care of me.

With the help of my Tanker buddies, I learned to take my mission seriously. I learned firsthand how my faithfulness can affect another's in the future.

Entrepreneurs are often responsible for crafting and leading the mission that others will commit their time and talents to. It is critical that we establish a high standard for both the direction and values our mission strives for. With this in mind, here are a few questions to ask yourself the next time you need to craft and execute a mission or project:

- Is the purpose and direction of the mission worthy of the time, resources and talents I am investing in it?

- Am I being consistent in my execution and clear in my communication of the mission and its objectives?

- Does my mission serve everyone involved, including our employees, customers, vendors, community, and leaders?

- How will I know when we are living out our mission objectives? What measures of success can we all agree to and seek after?

- Do I have the right people in the right places with the right skills to execute our mission? If not, how do I rework the mix to get there?

- Am I willing to be flexible to ensure we can accomplish our mission even if market conditions change dramatically?

- Are my skills best for executing our mission? If the time comes that my skills are inadequate, will I be willing to step aside for the good of the mission and our team? How will I know when the time comes?

- What is my plan for exiting when our mission is complete or when it makes sense to merge our efforts with someone else's?

There is a lot of talk in every company about strategic plans, market objectives, growth measurement, clarity of purpose, etc. All of these are simply elements of our basic mission. Before any of these issues matter, however, we as leaders must be clear about and committed to our mission and our team. All the rest is just details.

Know your mission and stay true to it!

Growing Forward

Take some time this week to consider some of the elements required to craft and execute your mission. Consider reviewing them with other company leaders to uncover any gaps and freshen your course moving forward.

Treasure This

"The things which you have heard from me in the presence of many witnesses, entrust these to faithful people who will be able to teach others also."
2 Timothy 2:2, NASB

"Peak performers see the ability to manage change as a necessity in fulfilling their missions."
Charles Garfield

"Here is the test to find whether your mission on earth is finished. If you're alive, it isn't."
Richard Bach

18

Exit Strategy

///

Win With a Solid Plan for a Great Finish

In many ways, entrepreneurs are like teenagers.

Both groups sometimes think and act like they are going to live forever. Most have very strong opinions about how the world works and their place in it. They even share a common belief that their predecessors somehow *just don't get it*. They perhaps entertain thoughts that the previous generation simply can't understand what they are going through because everything is so different now.

Each time I observe this mindset, it takes me back to my third-grade Sunday school class where I first heard about a man named King Solomon. Solomon was the son of King David (of David and Goliath fame) and was purported to be the richest and wisest man in the world 4,000 years ago. Among his many famous writings, one phrase perfectly fits this situation: "There is nothing new under the sun." In other words, everything we seek, see, learn, and understand is simply a reworking of previous knowledge. Pretty profound stuff for a guy who didn't even have an email address!

Considering that many of us don't appreciate or embrace this kind of precious wisdom as we could (or should) brings me to this assessment:

Entrepreneurs just don't know when to quit, stop, go back, or exit. By that I mean we find great joy in pushing ahead, overcoming, and tenaciously pursuing our goals, sometimes with sketchy plans and no real finish line in sight.

The reason we persist in these behaviors is simple. Most of the time it works for us—until it doesn't. When things start to fall apart, we begin to wake up to the fact that we missed something along the way. That something is called an "Exit Strategy."

You see, growing a business is like taking a road trip to somewhere we have never been before. If we don't know where we are going, any road will take us there. However, unlike a road trip to anywhere, a company is made up of people (employees, customers, vendors) who rapidly tire of asking "Are we there yet?" Since we have not really thought through the question, our only answer can be, "I don't know."

Having worked with hundreds of business owners, I can count on one hand those who started their companies with a detailed exit strategy in place. Most have suffered for not having one. But you don't have to.

Here are some things to consider as you work on putting an Exit Strategy in place:

- Just like in the 1970s game show Let's Make a Deal, when it comes to exiting your business, there are only three doors:
  » Door #1 – You die
  » Door #2 – Your business dies (runs out of money and closes down)
  » Door #3 – You sell your business (or give it to your kids)

» There is no Door #4 – you have to choose one of the first 3!

- Decide when enough is enough:
  » How big do you want to grow the company?
  » When will it become the most valuable to a potential buyer?
  » At what point does it stop being fun to operate?
  » What things are changing in the marketplace that will affect it?
  » Who are you mentoring to take it over someday?
  » What do you want to do with the rest of your life?

- Develop an Exit Strategy based on reality and adjust it regularly:
  » Decide which door you want to walk through – then don't look back
  » Network to find professionals who can help you build your plan
  » Routinely revise the plan to account for changes in your company and marketplace
  » Be flexible enough to move up or move back the implementation of your exit process
  » Talk through your "life after this company" plans with the important people in your life

When I think about developing an Exit Strategy, the words of a John Lennon song come to mind:

"Life is what happens to you while you are busy making other plans."

Growing Forward

Now might just be the perfect time to begin working on your exit strategy. Remember, it takes you a while to pull together all of the ideas, timelines, resources, and market intelligence you will need to put the plan into place. The sooner you start, the sooner you will have a handle on *which door* to choose.

Treasure This

"'For I know the plans I have for you,' declares the Lord, 'Plans to prosper you and not harm you, plans to give you hope and a future. Then you will call upon me and come and pray to Me, and I will listen to you. You will seek Me and find Me when you seek Me with all your heart.'"
Jeremiah 29:11-13, NASB

"The future is something which everyone reaches at the rate of sixty minutes an hour, whatever he does, whoever he is."
C.S. Lewis

"If one does not know to which port one is sailing, no wind is favorable."
Lucius Annaeus Seneca

SECTION THREE

DISCIPLINE

19

Focus

Embrace Your Future, Release Distractions

Entrepreneurs can be funny. Some are deeply creative, off-the-wall, outgoing, and downright entertaining. Others are studious, serious, goal-oriented, and introverted. Still others live and breathe to ingest great reams of facts and data. Most of these behaviors have more to do with individual personality types than the fact that they are trying to grow a thriving business.

All, however, share a common need. *The need to focus.* To center their minds on the activities and decisions that will drive their enterprises forward.

Sounds simple enough.

But after working with hundreds of entrepreneurs I have come to learn that for us leaders, focus is a really difficult state of mind to achieve and much less maintain all day, every day. Having studied this phenomenon for almost 40 years, I am still only able to draw one conclusion that makes sense to me.

Entrepreneurs are anatomically different from other people.

We are born with "sticky brains."

Let me explain what I mean by *sticky*.

My family and I live out in the country just west of Fort Worth, Texas. Our neighborhood is populated by horses, longhorn cattle, crickets, rattlesnakes, and field mice. While most of the varmints in our little ecosystem spend their time gobbling down their neighbors who are lower on the food chain than they are, field mice seem to get a pass somehow. That's the reason we have to use sticky mouse traps to capture and kill the little critters before they can come in and take over our house.

Last week, one of our Labrador Retrievers, Goliath, decided to investigate one of the glue traps. By the time I found him, he had the trap stuck securely to the right side of his big furry face. Two hours of clipping, cursing, and rinsing allowed me to un-stick my hound— but not before getting a heaping portion of the goop all over myself.

Just this morning, I think I finally removed the last remnants of our sticky little adventure from my right leg (I hope).

When I say we entrepreneurs have "sticky brains," I mean that everywhere we go, everything we see, hear, taste, smell, touch, or remember somehow ends up stuck to our brain like it was a glue trap. We can walk through a completely empty room and come out the other side with 10 new ideas. We can go on vacation to "forget about work" and come back with 50 new business cards from total strangers we are sure will help our business someday. We can go to a movie and find ourselves writing to-do notes on the side of the popcorn container. Post-it notes choke our desks, dashboards, bathroom counters, and kitchen cabinets. For us, ideas stick to our brains like mice to a glue trap.

I'm not saying that this is particularly bad or destructive behavior. It's simply who we are. What I am saying is that knowing our brains are sticky tells us a lot about why it is often so hard for us to focus.

This special ability to grab inspiration out of thin air makes us great at what we do, but it can also be the thing that holds us back.
To make our situation even worse, we live in a world that seems to be divided into two opposing schools of thought concerning making decisions.

One school says, "You had better look before you leap"—better to err on the side of caution.

The other school says, "If you hesitate, you are lost"—better to take a chance than to let the opportunity pass you by.

As entrepreneurs, we are forced to live between these two polar opposites and still stay focused on making sound decisions over and over again.

There are many reasons why gifted managers and leaders don't succeed in launching or growing successful businesses. I believe that not recognizing the importance and difficulty of *remaining focused* may be the single biggest reason for our failures.

Focus on the little things, and the big things will take care of themselves!

Growing Forward

Take some time this week to focus on which areas of your business and personal life could use a little more structured attention. Then, with your brain wrapped in wax paper for protection from distractions, make a short list of goals that you can commit to working on over the next 30 days. You may be surprised at how far your ideas can go on when nothing else is sticking to them!

Treasure This

"The plans of the diligent lead to profit as surely as haste leads to poverty."
Proverbs 21:5, NIV

"You can't depend on your judgment when your imagination is out of focus."
Mark Twain

"Never neglect details. When everyone's mind is dulled or distracted, the leader must be doubly vigilant."
Colin Powell

20

Choices

Once a Choice is Made, the Choice Controls the Chooser

Driving to work this morning, I heard a story on the radio about a farmer who had a little too much time on his hands while waiting for the corn to ripen in his fields. Since he had just purchased a new tractor and was dying to use it for the first time, he decided to drive it over to the other side of his farm, where there was a tall stand of wheat waiting to be cut down.

Somewhere along the way, he got the notion that it would be great fun to cut a maze in the middle of the tallest wheat (a maze in the maize). After several hours, he found he had done such a good job, he was totally and hopelessly lost inside his own creation. Tired and frustrated, he finally had to cut a path out of the maze to find his way back to the barn.

This story struck me as both funny and painfully familiar.

How often have I allowed boredom, lack of discipline, or just plain ignorance to drive me toward making bad choices? When was the last time I lost sight of my goals and dreams? Maybe this sounds familiar to you, too. Do you ever fall victim to the maze of circumstances that seem to grow up around us as we sleep—haunting our dreams and distracting us when we wake?

I don't believe our lives are supposed to be a series of random, unrelated circumstances that conspire to rob us of our peace and sabotage our happiness. Rather, life is a series of choices we make. Think of it as a trail we walk, sometimes alone, sometimes with others, but always directly reflecting the choices we have made—choices that often seem right at the time, based on what we understand or are hoping for.

Walking through this continual maze of life, making choices, and reacting to the people and circumstances around us defines the human condition. We are often forced to make serious choices that will dictate our future opportunities—while knowing we are making them with incomplete information or an inappropriate mindset.

While this is a somewhat sloppy process that often frustrates us as individuals, it can be catastrophic for us as leaders in our organizations.

Being constantly confronted with choices that will affect the lives of everyone in our sphere of influence brings with it a high level of stress and anxiety. Add to this the additional influences of competitive pressures, company politics, and personal goals, and it is easy to understand why so many executives struggle to cope.

As leaders, we seldom have all of the facts at hand to render completely reliable decisions. It is for this reason that we need to base our choices on certain time-honored practices, including:

- Trust your gut—your own life experiences provide valuable insight into many situations.
- Seek out the counsel of others who have no material interest in the outcome—peer mentoring groups are a valuable resource in this regard.

- Develop a cadre of trusted employees, customers, and vendors that will give you frank and honest feedback while keeping information to themselves.

- Develop viable alternatives to fall back on if your decisions are not 100% on target, and be quick to recognize the need to make adjustments.

- Don't exaggerate the issue or the outcome—people want the facts, and they will respect your honesty.

- Relax—understand that your goal is not perfection; your goal is consistency and integrity.

- Be confident—others read more into how you act out your decisions than simply what you say.

- Lead from the front—be the first to incorporate new decisions into your process going forward. This kind of modeling can powerfully instill confidence in your team.

We all know that there is no magic that will make all of our choices and decisions work well in every situation, but with practice and introspection, we can develop a trustworthy process for making them.

Always remember that not choosing is a choice!

Growing Forward

Take time this week to consider some of the important choices that you need to make. Incorporate several of these suggestions into your decision-making process. With a little determination, maybe in the future, you can cut down on the time spent in the maze of difficult choices!

Treasure This

"But if any of you lacks wisdom, let him ask of God, who gives to all generously and without reproach, and it will be given to him."
James 1:5, NASB

"Be sure you put your feet in the right place, then stand firm."
Abraham Lincoln

"If you limit your choices only to what seems possible or reasonable, you disconnect yourself from what you truly want, and all that is left is compromise."
Robert Fritz

21

Balance

The Ultimate Prize Worth Winning

I like barber shops.

I like almost everything about them—the way they smell, the way they look, the way the bench is kind of worn down where guys have been sanding it with their butts for the last forty years while waiting for a haircut. I particularly like the way a man sits up high in the chair when it is his turn. Yes, I really like barber shops.

What I have not always liked are the barbers that work there. At times, I have had to listen to angry and bitter men complain about the problems or lack of opportunities that have *forced* them to work as a barber (a profession which I greatly admire).

That is until I met Gary.

Gary loved being a barber. He started barbering back in 1955 (the year I was born) and just recently retired after 52 years of faithful service to multiple generations of grateful patrons. Gary cut my hair every other week for over ten years. During that time, we got to really know each other, and I looked forward to our time together.

It turns out that not only did Gary barber full time, but he also ran 30-50 head of black Angus cattle on his 30-acre spread out north of town. He was also a Deacon at the local Baptist church where he taught Sunday school, visited the widows who were unable to get out to church, and drove the bus to pick up the country kids every week. Gary had a very full and balanced life.

Over the years, I never heard Gary say a disparaging word about anything or anybody. He was always very friendly and seemed to genuinely love cutting hair. One day, I asked him why he was always so happy. His answer was short and to the point: "Two reasons, Tony. First, because I love Jesus, and I know that he loves me. Second, my Bible says that God owns the cattle on a thousand hills. The way I figure it, any time I have a need, all he has to do is sell a few head of them cattle and I'm all fixed up!" That was Gary all the way—straight up with the answer to your question and a free smile thrown in just to make you glad you asked.

Gary was a good barber, but he was a great role model and teacher. Thanks, Gary.

I believe that living a balanced life is all about learning to be who we really are and pursuing the people, opportunities, and challenges that will keep us in that place of fulfillment and usefulness.

Over the years, people like Gary have encouraged me to continue in my pursuit of a balanced life. I will confess that it has often been a real struggle. There are many reasons, but the main one is that the whole concept of balance is just so big! I mean just think about it.

The notion of balanced living encompasses what we do with our time, as well as how, where, and when we work, worship, and play. It determines how we spend or invest our money and volunteer our talents. It dictates our level of commitment to a certain political view or religious doctrine. It is influenced by how we were raised and will seriously impact our children and their future —for better or worse. It is sometimes totally in our control, but just as often, it is a complete prisoner of our choices and circumstances.

I have found that setting priorities that help me live in balance routinely means turning down opportunities and saying no to very sincere and persuasive people. In fact, to become really proficient at this process has required years of practice. In that time, I have learned several important principles, including:

- Experience and practice teach us when to pass up good opportunities in order to be prepared for the *great ones* that come along with patience (the great opportunities reinforce balanced living rather than detracting from it).

- A growing lack of interest in our spiritual life, friendships, and physical health is an indicator that our life is spinning out of balance.

- Choosing to be accountable to our family and a few close friends is our best assurance that we will make choices that support a balanced lifestyle.

- Living a balanced life requires us to learn to be content with having our needs (not necessarily all of our wants) met.

- Living in balance will often find us debating the value of seeking more achievements, accolades, and money for our work (spelled "selling out to our jobs") vs. pursuing the simple gratification that comes with doing our jobs well.

So if we know that living our lives in balance is this challenging, then why even try? After all, it does not seem to be all that common. Most folks spend their time "getting all they can, canning all they get, and sitting on the can." I think this has also been referred to as *The Rat Race* or *Keeping up with the Joneses*.

Allow me to give you a few reasons why I believe that living life in balance is the *ultimate prize worth winning*.

Living a balanced life...

- Helps our body, mind, and spirit operate at their peak of performance and in unison.

- Lets us be who we really are and not have to put on a front for other people.

- Helps us define where we fit in the world and gives us a sense of belonging.

- Gives us the time we need to rest, recreate, and reflect on the world around us.

- Builds our faith and strengthens our desire and ability to serve others in need.

- Teaches us to live in the moment rather than constantly striving for the future.

- Makes us an active participant in raising our children instead of a distant spectator.

As a serial entrepreneur, I have had a front-row seat to observe literally hundreds of other executives and co-workers. My observation is that no matter what level of responsibility a person holds in an organization, their effectiveness is greatly enhanced or diminished based on how they live their whole life. Those who have learned to balance their spiritual, family, and professional interests seem always to outperform and outlast their out-of-balance peers.

Success or Failure may be out of our control, but Balance is our choice!

Growing Forward

This week, take some time to examine how you spend your time, talents, and resources. Start figuring out what activities and interests are helping or hurting your balance. Put in the time it takes to get real about who you are and what you want out of life. Then, seek out family and friends who can help you regain and maintain that balance. You may even want to hire an Executive Coach to help you accelerate the learning.

Treasure This

"But seek ye first the kingdom of God, and his righteousness; and all these things shall be added unto you."
Matthew 6:33, KJV

"One school of thought says, 'You had better look before you leap.' The other says, 'If you hesitate, you are lost.' All of life must be lived in balance between these two poles."
Larry Ragland

"Fortunate indeed is the man who takes exactly the right measure of himself, and holds a just balance between what he can acquire and what he can use."
Peter Mere Latham

22

Opportunities

———————————— // ————————————

All Are Not the Same, All Are Not for You

Mornings at our house are very predictable. We roll out of bed, get our coffee, and go out to the backyard to let our golden labs Samson and Goliath out of their kennel. From that point on, until we go to work, they pretty much run the show.

First comes the feeding, then the dog biscuits, then the chew bones. Finally, with full tummies, they lie down and go back to sleep. All along we are sitting on the back porch drinking our coffee and looking out on the pastures of North Texas filled with horses and long horned cattle. It is our daily ritual and we love it.

One Saturday, this little rendezvous with our furry friends was disrupted by an unexpected visitor in the form of a small gray field mouse. Midway through their chow time, the dogs spotted the little fellow dashing past their food bowls. The ensuing chases upended chairs, turned over potted plants, and generally turned our serene back porch into a war zone.

Millions of years of genetic mapping combined to bring about a quick end to the hunt. Our hounds (both full-blood retrievers weighing close to 100 pounds) made quick work of "pack hunting" Mr. Mouse. Once the chase was over, the boys chose to leave him on our back porch as a trophy and reminder of their outstanding hunting abilities. While I was ok with temporarily humoring their need to celebrate the victorious pursuit, my wife Jane was not — so I toted the mouse out to our back field and committed him back to the circle of life.

When I returned to finish my coffee I noticed after every ten minutes or so the dogs would put their noses down and retrace the path of the hunt. They did this at least three times while I was there and even a few more times the next day.

Their strange behavior got me thinking. For Samson and Goliath, that mouse was a huge opportunity to use their natural gifts (after all, they are hunting dogs). But once the hunt (opportunity) was finished, they kept replaying it, reliving it, even dreaming about it over and over again.

While pondering this process, I could not help but think of myself and other entrepreneurs I have known. We find an opportunity that allows us to use our best skill and abilities, then we pursue it vigorously. If our efforts prove to be fruitful, we invest tremendous time and energy looking for that type of opportunity again.

But opportunities are like mice. They show up quickly from places we don't expect and then they are gone —often forever.

As entrepreneurs, we get caught in the trap of wasting valuable time and resources trying to make opportunities reappear artificially. We repeat previous behaviors (good and bad) in the hope that lightning will strike twice in the same place. I have done this myself, with little success.

As I look back, I see much of our successes in the past have been a matter of circumstances and people seeking us out as they have become aware of our particular skills or experience. It is for this reason that I suggest we decide ahead of time what kinds of work or projects we really want to do. With these decisions made, we can position ourselves to take advantage of new opportunities as they present themselves.

Some of the ways I have found useful in preparing myself for these prospects are:

- Networking — Discipline yourself to attend networking events and maintain consistent contact with previous customers, vendors, and industry contacts. Never miss the chance to give a congratulatory phone call or email when someone gets promoted or closes a big deal.

- Ongoing training — When an opportunity arises it is critical that our skills and knowledge be equal to the task at hand. Current information and understanding are the new currency of business. Lifelong learning is no longer an option — it is a requirement for success.

- Volunteering — In a world with so many resources, there still seems to be a greater and greater need. Becoming a volunteer, mentor, or community board member not only allows us to give back to our society, it also positions us to relate to other professionals outside of our industry in a meaningful way. These interactions enhance our knowledge, build our reputation, and keep us correctly grounded to what is important in life.

- Sensitivity — We have all heard the expression "Opportunity knocks," but in my experience, it seems to just "beep the horn" as it drives by. We have to be paying close attention to take full advantage of opportunities that come into our lives. Proactively balancing our professional, family, and spiritual lives can help us become more sensitive.

Make sure "The prize is worth eating the Cracker Jacks" before you start!

Growing Forward

Take some time this week to review your current opportunities with these concepts in mind. If you find you are "chasing the same mouse" as before, make some new commitments and redirect your efforts. Oh, and it wouldn't be a bad idea to get some input from your people in the process— one more opportunity to build your team.

Treasure This

"...Making the most of every opportunity in these evil days."
Ephesians 5:16, NIV

"We are all faced with a series of great opportunities, brilliantly disguised as impossible situations."
Charles R. Swindoll

"Opportunity is missed by most people because it is dressed in overalls and looks like work."
Thomas Edison

23

Discernment

The Discipline that Empowers Great Choices

In act I, scene 3 of Hamlet, Polonius speaks to his son Laertes as he prepares for a trip away from home. His instruction: "To thine own self be true."

More recently someone at a Madison Avenue advertising firm wrote: "Choosy mothers choose Jif."

So what does Shakesphere have in common with peanut butter? Where exactly does the intersection of this timeless prose and crass American commercialism occur?

In a word, the intersection falls at the place of discernment: the ability to accurately identify what is and is not right for your life, your family, or your business.

A prime example of this principle I learned by observing my faithful hounds Samson and Goliath. You see, even though they are simple canines with brains the size of a walnut, they are also very consistent about what they will and will not hunt (and ultimately eat).

Their list of favorite hunts includes: rabbits, squirrels, cats (particularly very slow ones), birds, rodents, possums, crickets, coyotes and other assorted small varmints.

The roster of things they ignore is populated by: snakes, amphibians, grasshoppers, spiders, other dogs (out of professional courtesy, no doubt), and assorted large varmints (especially those with long horns).

Having cared for these dogs since they were puppies, I can tell you it took them a while (and a lot of lost fur/chewed up ears) to determine which creatures made it to each of their lists. The snakes and longhorns were easy picks for the "no-go" category as were the rabbits and squirrels for the "let's do lunch… again" group. Experience, both good and bad, seems to have had more to do with their ability to make these selections than millions of years of breeding ever could.

So how do we as leaders become discerning in our choices and decisions?

It begins when we are honest with ourselves about what our natural gifts and passions are and are not. While most of us become pretty good at adapting to the world around us in this regard, we are nevertheless equipped from birth with certain skill sets and loves, which if nourished, will take us down the road of excellence and fulfillment.

Here are some ways to identify and amplify these natural attributes:

- Take a "Passion Inventory" — list out on a sheet of paper all of the kinds of projects you would do just for the fun and learning involved, not for the money.
- Take a "Present State Inventory" — on another sheet of paper, list all of your current work, hobbies, and interests.
- Compare notes — make a third list of both similarities and differences between your passions and your present state.

These are the areas you will need to re-align. In order to reach your passions and better invest your time in the future, you'll need to become more selective.

- Make a plan— Using these lists, look out over the next one, three, and five years and start finding ways to move in the direction of your passions. If this is done consistently, you may find your view of future retirement does not include leaving the workforce. Rather it may simply mean moving into work you find more meaningful and significant, work that you select to fuel your passions.

Trust your own history about what you truly are passionate about—and what you are not!

Growing Forward

Just as Polonius felt about being true to self, just like mothers choose to be picky about what their kids eat, just the way Samson and Goliath live their lives as conditioned carnivores, you must choose discernment to live a purposeful and fulfilling life!

Treasure This

"Do not be conformed to this world, but be transformed by the renewal of your mind, that by testing you may discern what is the will of God, what is good and acceptable and perfect."
Romans 12:2, ESV

"So complex is the human spirit that it can itself scarce discern the deep springs which impel it to action."
Arthur Conan Doyle, Author of "Sherlock Holmes"

"He who knows others is clever; He who knows himself has discernment."
Laozi

24

Tools

Mastering Our Craft

It's early Saturday morning, and I am really excited. I am hours away from finishing a complicated woodworking project on my new workbench. This beauty is made out of hard rock maple, has two large vices, and boasts an assortment of drawers and shelves to store my best saws and chisels. Building this piece has been an educational and emotional experience.

What really makes this workbench so special to me is that it has a lot of me built into it—literally. I say this because I have sweat and bled on almost every part of it. Now, if you have ever done much woodworking, you know that bleeding on a project is just part of the process. At least in my case, it is almost a required function in order to bring it to completion. In fact, you can often sort out the hard-core professional woodworkers from the rookies by looking at their hands. The pros tend to have seriously scarred-up hands and missing fingers. Fortunately for me—even after 40 years of woodworking—I still possess all of my digits. Still, just in case, I keep a well-stocked first aid kit close at hand!

Another thing separating the professional craftsman from the weekend sawdust junkies is their commitment to gaining skills with their tools. Professionals are very proficient in the use of wood chisels, hand saws, and hand planes. Hundreds of hours of practice are required to master and maintain these tools. Professionals also know that attention to detail is critical. It is for this reason that pros measure twice and cut once. Time and experience have taught them that a few extra seconds spent double-checking the measurement of a cut keeps a lot of really good wood out of the waste bin.

Compare this standard with the mindset of many rookie woodworkers who believe *sandpaper* is a precision tool and a proper substitute for almost every cutting function in the shop. Their limited skills force them to cut each piece of wood just a little too large and then sand it down to size. This is not woodworking, it is *wood grinding*, and its practice prevents the plebe from ever perfecting his tool skills.

Poor tool skills are not limited to the woodshop. This phenomenon exists in almost every department of every company in the world to some degree. The reasons people ignore or choose not to master the tools of their trade are many and often correctable. If enough company employees fail to gain and maintain mastery of their tools, the business may not remain competitive or even survive. Here are some ways to ensure people, processes, and tools will always be razor sharp:

- Constantly evaluate your systems —Employees will often take the path of least resistance when it comes to executing assigned duties. Continually monitor every critical system (sales performance, inventory control, financial accounting, product rotation, loss prevention, internet use, etc.) to determine if each is being used properly or if people have found ways to subvert it.

- If it ain't broke, break it—Routinely ask, "How can we do this better?" Focus on high-value activities (raising profit margins, managing employee turnover issues, developing more effective training, evaluating your place in the market space, etc.). Do not ignore the processes that already work well. Everything changes constantly; everything can be improved continually.

- Listen to your business—Schedule monthly brown-bag lunches when your employees can sit with you in a room, eat their lunch and tell you what is happening in their departments. This is an owner-employee function with no department managers present. Bring a blank yellow pad, listen, and take lots of notes. Only talk in order to ask questions or answer them, and keep your answers short. What you learn will become your new tool improvement list.

- Reward proficiency—For every function or process in your company, there is probably at least one employee who has learned to master it. Make it a practice to routinely recognize and reward craftsmanship of this kind. Then, ask that employee to mentor someone else in the process. Not only will your people learn to function more efficiently, they will also grow to appreciate and honor each other's tool skills.

- Model craftsmanship—As the leader of the enterprise, you are under constant observation by your team. Take every opportunity to demonstrate your mastery of company business functions. Invest time on the shop floor of each department. Work side by side with your first-line employees and customers to demonstrate your personal commitment to individual performance excellence.

In every business, as in every woodworking shop, there are masters, and there are apprentices. Both are students on a journey to become the best they can be at their trade. Every interaction between them is an opportunity to learn and progress toward a common goal: excellence. As leaders, we must initiate these cooperative learning experiences.

When we initiate learning, we perpetuate an age-old tradition as masters of our craft.

Growing Forward

Take some time this week to remember back to when you had to know how to do practically everything in your company. For some of you, this is still the case – good for you! Either way, make a list of critical functions that have the most effect on the health and growth of your business on a daily basis. Then, schedule time to work side by side with the employees who perform those tasks. Finally, when you are with them, listen and determine if they still have the right tools to do that job. If so, great—move on. If not, provide them with the new tools and training they need to succeed.

Treasure This

"For we are His workmanship, created in Christ Jesus for good works, which God prepared beforehand so that we would walk in them."
Ephesians 2:10, NASB

"You can't expect to meet the challenges of today with yesterday's tools and expect to be in business tomorrow."
Author unknown

"The stone age was marked by man's clever use of crude tools; the information age, to date, has been marked by man's crude use of clever tools."
Author unknown

25

Transparency

One Set of Rules for Everyone

Over a lifetime of starting new businesses and consulting for others, I have heard the word transparency used with great frequency. In fact, I have almost relegated it to that pile of 'nothing words' that include vis-a-vis, ergo, clearly, quintessential and empowerment. These are all words that used to mean something but are now so overused, misused or misunderstood they have become nonsensical.

I said "almost" because I believe the word transparency and the concept it conveys is worth saving and maybe even rehabilitating.

For entrepreneurs, owners, or leaders in general, transparency can be a very threatening prescription for change. The basic idea of allowing others to see us as we really are may actually be a totally original notion for some. For me, moving from the stereotypical top-down management style that dominates most organizations to one set of rules for everyone (owners and managers included) was quite a shock to the system. But it has totally and positively transformed our company while enriching my experience as an owner.

In a transparent company, the highest value is respect. This fleshes itself out in many forms:

- Access—When we designed our new building, we kept the management, sales and distribution center on one level (it would have been more cost-effective to put the management offices upstairs). To be transparent, we first have to be accessible and not placed in an ivory tower of sorts.

- Architecture—Every person who has leadership responsibilities at our company has at least one 4'x 8' window facing the inside of the building toward our employee workspaces. This was arranged not to allow leaders to watch others as they work but to allow employees to watch their leaders and to ensure we are doing our jobs to move the company (and their dreams) forward.

- Rules—Ever wonder why, after having worked hard to hire really bright, talented people, business owners bury them in rules and policies that scream, "You have to be really stupid to work here and put up with this stuff"? The short answer is that most rules are the result of some bad experience the owner had while running the business. It is simple cause and effect. An employee, customer, or vendor takes advantage of the owner and BAM! We have a new rule to keep that from ever happening again. In a transparent company, owners constantly review the systems to make sure that only absolutely required rules are kept in effect. Without this vigilance, excessive rules eventually suffocate the most creative contributors in the organization. The owner's first job is to keep it transparent.

- Authenticity—As an owner, I bring my own problems and personality deficiencies to my job. When I make a really bad decision, lose my temper, or simply say something inappropriate, it is my responsibility to come clean before my employees. Since I expect them to tell me the truth, how can I exempt myself when I fail them? Authenticity is the thread with which a transparent entrepreneur weaves a long-lasting tapestry with employees, customers and vendors.

When we as leaders choose to create an environment that rewards transparency and holds us to the same standard, it frees the people around us to relax and be their best. As this group of people comes together to solve problems and grow the company, it is nothing short of amazing how much fun and profits improve.

It is our job to model transparency for our people!

Growing Forward

This week, take a hard look in the mirror. All of the large and small imperfections you see are not hidden from your people. Even more, they know your heart by the way you speak and act. Today might be a good day to start reworking your company into a more transparent place. Remember, the first move is yours!

Treasure This

"For if anyone is a hearer of the word and not a doer, he is like a man who looks at his natural face in a mirror; for once he has looked at himself and gone away, he has immediately forgotten what kind of person he was."
James 1:23-24, NASB

"Great leadership does not mean running away from reality. Sometimes the hard truths might just demoralize the company, but at other times sharing difficulties can inspire people to take action that will make the situation better."
John Kotter

"You don't lead by hitting people over the head – that's assault, not leadership."
Dwight David Eisenhower

26

Goals

Learning to Be Optimistically Realistic

The parched, barren prairie stretches out for limitless miles in all directions. The gusty, dirty wind perpetually roars in our faces with the intensity of a hellfire and damnation preacher making his final appeal for souls at a West Texas tent revival. Many have already fainted away, others have had heart attacks, and one or two will die. Like me, however, the remnant who remains have moved past the pain and discouragement and into their own heads. Here, even the metronome beat and sting of dripping sweat in our eyes no longer registers in our overheated brains. Here, simply finishing is a win!

Welcome to Wichita Falls, Texas. Welcome to the Hotter than Hell 100.

The Hotter than Hell 100 Bicycle Race is an annual event that attracts over 18,000 athletes each year—cyclists who choose to pit their physical and mental stamina against the worst conditions Texas has to offer. Simply put, the weather is bad (as in HOT!), the wind blows into your face for the 50 miles out into the country *and* for the miserable 50 miles back. The roads are primarily tar and gravel black top, constantly shimmering and weeping a slick, molten ooze. These road conditions conspire with the close proximity of every semi-comatose rider to produce some serious pile-ups along the course.

I have ridden the Hotter than Hell twice for two different reasons.

The first time I took part in the race was about a year after my Dad (my best friend) died. I was 35 years old and had made it my goal to begin living up to the legacy he had passed on to me. Dad invested his life in people, and I wanted to do the same. At the time of his death, my wife Jane and I had two young boys, Michael (age 5) and Daniel (age 1). I was about 50 pounds overweight and out of shape. I knew I needed to make some serious changes if I expected to see my grandchildren someday. Since we lived in an area surrounded by miles and miles of country roads, I chose bicycling as my aerobic activity. That, along with careful eating and consistent encouragement from Jane, prepared me for my first 100-mile race. This ride was a tribute to my Dad.

The second time I rode (the very next year) was mainly to prove to myself that I could do it again. The first time I rode to look back on all Dad had taught me; this time, I rode as the new leader of the Ford clan and the guy who was now responsible to set an example for my own boys. The second ride was for me.

I share this story because it gets to the heart of what goal-setting is all about: looking into the future at something we want and then taking the steps necessary to go after it. Since there are so many excellent books written about the mechanics of goal-setting, I won't go into it here. What I do want you to remember is how important it is to fully understand why we need goals and that we must commit to them fully if we expect serious, positive results. Here are some areas of life where having solid goals will make a real difference:

- Personal goals help us become more than we are now—more healthy, more skilled, more aware, and more fulfilled.

- Family goals bring us together around common interests and build strong bonds. I highly recommend camping together as a first step in this process. Even the simple task of erecting a tent can be a real goal-setting eye-opener.

- Business goals help us fulfill our responsibilities to our employees, customers, and vendors. They have a way of binding us to these folks in a common struggle to become successful. Our mutual interdependence makes us all better.

- Short-term goals allow us to celebrate our successes with the people closest to us. We need this continuing encouragement to move forward and stay motivated.

- Medium-term goals act as our road map to the future. Without taking time to routinely check in on how we are doing, it is easy to end up way off course.

- Long-term goals remind us that each time we succeed, we are building a valuable legacy that others can follow. These goals are the ones that ultimately determine how we finish the race.

Over the years, I have observed all kinds of people set goals and then go after attaining them. Almost everyone starts out the same way — with great intentions, good, solid plans, and lots of enthusiasm and energy. Few finish well.

By that I mean only a small percentage of us keep our focus on our long-term goals and thereby become the person we want to be. Basically, we allow ourselves to be redirected away from where we want to go in life. The key to reaching our goal is always to remember this is our life, the only one we get and we are the stewards of it.

Be bold! Make it your goal to be just a little better than the best.

Growing Forward

Ever heard the expression, "If you don't know where you are going, any road will do"? It means that without a specific destination in mind (a goal), you will simply end up where you end up—whether for good or not so good. Take time this week to examine where your life is headed and ask yourself, "Where do I want my life to take me, and what difference do I want to make?" Your answers will become the first step down a new road filled with greater enjoyment and significant living!

On another note, I chose to ride both of my "Hotter than Hell 100" races on a mountain bike instead of a road bike (much slower and more pedaling), just to make it interesting. Needless to say, I got a lot of "Now *that guy* is crazy" looks along the way. But hey, what's the point of setting the same goals as everyone else?

Treasure This

"Not that I have already grasped it all or have already become perfect, but I press on if I may also take hold of that for which I was even taken hold of by Christ Jesus."
Philippians 3:12, NASB

"You are never too old to set another goal or to dream a new dream."
C.S. Lewis

"My goal in life is to become as wonderful as my dog thinks I am."
Author unknown – but I wish it had been me!

27

Planning or Procrastinating

Knowing the Difference is Everything

"When we works, we works, and when we sits, we sits. And we don't confuse the two!"

My favorite mentor, Larry Ragland, loved to share this expression with me when he thought I was overthinking a problem or taking too much time to complete a project.

His point was that work requires us to focus, plan, and execute, normally on some type of time schedule, while sitting, resting, and enjoying hobbies and entertainment can be done any way we choose. Neither one is better or worse, but for sure they are very different activities that should never be confused with each other.

And so it is when we tell ourselves we are planning something when in fact we are simply putting it off or denying it.

For example, have you ever heard yourself say, "I am planning to do that just as soon as _____"? You can probably fill in the blank.

Looking back over the years, I now know when I used that expression, what I really meant to say was, "I will do that thing if and only IF I have exhausted all other options and excuses" (*and* maybe have a gun pointed at my head).

This book you're holding is another example. For over 20 years people have told me, "Tony, you should really put those ideas into a book so other folks could benefit from them." To which I would reply, "Maybe when things slow down a little I will." Well, here I am (at 68) finally committing these concepts to paper, even though my life is just as busy as it's ever been.

So what changed?

For me, I finally got my brain wrapped around the idea that, as busy entrepreneurs, we often allow planning to degenerate into procrastination. This decline means we waste precious time in serious denial and avoidance behavior (never hard for most of us to do). We falsely believe someday our situation will improve and allow us to follow through on our plans. As it turns out, I ultimately ran out of reasons (spelled excuses) for not writing this book. Bad Tony!

Keeping in mind how easily planning can morph into procrastination, here are some questions I have learned to ask myself to ensure I am really planning for future successes and not just avoiding difficult issues:

- When will this plan be needed? If the plans you are making today are not going to be implemented in the near future, why make them? While it is good to have a five-year plan, it is much more important to have a firm grasp on what is going to happen in the next five days and weeks. Be careful not to sacrifice too much time and brain power dreaming and scheming at the expense of solid, near-term, profit-producing ideas.

- How will this plan move us forward? Often when it comes to planning, we are quick to answer the question of "what" but slow to understand the full implications of short, medium, and long-term plan benefits (the *why*). Just as for every action, there is an equal and opposite reaction (Newton's Third Law of Physics), for every plan, there are a variety of opportunity costs to be carefully weighed against the benefits offered. Pay particular attention to how the costs associated with growing top-line sales are affecting the growth or decline of bottom line profits. Remember to pay attention to outcomes, or you may plan yourself right out of business.

- How often do we stop and re-evaluate the plan? Just as a husband cannot simply tell his wife "I love you" on their wedding day and expect her to remain convinced of that fact until he tells her otherwise, so it is with revisiting our plans. Marriages and businesses are both living things and they do not exist in a vacuum. For any long-term plan to succeed, it requires stakeholders to pause on a routine basis to examine and discuss all the changes that have occurred since the plan was created. Companies and couples that make this discipline a regular practice tend to be much more satisfied and successful.

- When is it time to make a new plan or exit? Plans are only as good as the information and environment they are based on. Over time, if either changes significantly, the plan may simply stop working. Many companies fail because their leaders do not recognize and react quickly enough to dramatic changes in their industry or market segment. It is for this reason companies should start out with exit strategies that include a number of "what if" scenarios designed to take these potential changes into account.

Remember, great planning results in measurable outcomes within a desirable timeframe. Procrastination results in wasted time, multiplied anxiety, and broken relations.

The choice is yours!

Growing Forward

Planning is best accomplished in an atmosphere of limited distractions where you and your team can relax and focus on the future. Take some time this week to schedule a get away with your people and make a plan for taking the company to its next level. You may be amazed at what great plans you can come up with together!

Treasure This

"I know the plans I have for you, declares the LORD. They are plans for peace and not disaster, plans to give you a future filled with hope."
Jeremiah 29:11, NIV

"Procrastination is suicide on the installment plan."
Author unknown

"Good fortune is what happens when opportunity meets with planning."
Thomas Alva Edison

SECTION FOUR

CHALLENGES

28

Tenacity

Finishing What We Start, Enduring Till the End

Think back over your life. Was there a challenge, project, relationship or job that just was not your thing? Anything you were just horrible at doing?

For me, it was high school football.

In 1970, my family lived in Lawton, Oklahoma. My Dad had just returned from Vietnam and was stationed at Fort Sill. As a 6'4" 245 lbs. freshman, I was deeply aware of my town's expectation that I would play football. I had just started at the brand new MacArthur High School and I joined the team.

Having spent the last three years in Germany playing soccer ("football" in that part of the world), I was not very familiar with the rules of American Football, so my first month of two-a-day summer practices was a constant reminder of my own ignorance. In spite of the never-ending stream of verbal abuse that rained down on me every day, I persisted until I finally understood the ins and outs of the game.

My next challenge was to try and decipher what all of the Xs and Os meant in the playbooks. Since I had no experience with the game, it took another month to figure out exactly where my position (right tackle) appeared on the diagrams. This journey of exploration invited further comments on my apparent lack of intelligence and a continuing barrage of insults questioning my lineage.

By the time the first season rolled around, it became clear that even though I now understood the rules and plays, I was simply *slow*. But this did not stop my coach from trying to encourage me. He was fond of saying, "Ford, you run faster than any fat kid I have ever seen." Talk about a backhanded compliment!

As the season came and went, I found myself spending two hours every afternoon at practice holding the tackling dummy while the starting players devised new and creative ways to miss it and hit me. I played a total of three quarters that year, always at the end of games when we were at least 40 points ahead and the other team had given up all hope.

Seasons two and three were carbon copies of the first. But through every single season, in spite of cold and miserable weather, my Dad came to every game, knowing I would not play. His encouragement kept me from giving up.

At the end of our third season, the team had won all of its games and we were scheduled to play in the Class 1A state championship game in Davis, Oklahoma. But there was a problem. Since we were a new school with no booster club, we didn't have the money to pay for the bus to get us to Davis. So the coaches got together and organized a chili supper event to raise money.

What happened next taught me my first real lesson about the power of tenacity. The head coach gathered up the eight of us players who were either third or fourth-string guys. He sat us down in the locker room and said; "Boys, we are going to have a chili supper to raise money for the bus to Davis. The tickets are $2.00 each. Whoever sells the most tickets—I will make a Letterman this year."

I could not believe my own ears. Here I was with a total of three quarters played this year (it took a minimum of 12 to letter) and I was being given a shot at my own letter jacket. At that moment, I committed myself to the task of selling more tickets than anyone else.

For the next week, I spent every spare minute I had going door to door peddling my tickets. We were in the middle of a cold spell, and on two of the days the temperature was in the mid-teens with sleet coming down. When folks opened their doors, I guess I looked so pitiful that they just could not help but buy some tickets (in the hope that I would not die right there on their doorstep).

Sure enough, when the time came to tally up the ticket sales, I had sold over $800 worth, while my nearest competitor had only sold $200. I had finally earned my letter jacket!

I share this story with you to make a point.

Often, we discover our true gifts and abilities in the midst of our greatest challenges and disappointments. Tenacity is the fuel that allows us to keep moving through life when it seems we will never find the right fit.

Tenacity is sometimes all we have when there are no new ideas or answers to move us forward. It is unexplainably supported by those around us who love us for who we are, not simply for what we do. For me, that person was my Dad.

Tenacity is a deep well within each of us. If we take the time to fill it with good health practices, rich relationships, and challenging dreams for the future, it will always be there to sustain us as we move out of our failures and into our successes.

Never give up. I say again, never, never, never give up!

Growing Forward

Take some time this week to think about the things in life that really challenge you. It may be a health issue, competitive pressures, finances, etc. Choose one of these situations and really sink your teeth into it. Determine to work through it until it is resolved. Then, use the satisfaction you get from that victory to move on to the next, less pressing issue.

Treasure This

"Not that I have already obtained all this [Christ-likeness], or have already been made perfect, but I press on to take hold of that for which Christ Jesus took hold of me. Brothers, I do not consider myself yet to have taken hold of it. But one thing I do: forgetting what is behind and straining toward what is ahead, I press on toward the goal to win the prize for which God has called me Heavenward in Christ Jesus."
Philippians 3:12-14, NIV

"By perseverance the snail reached the ark."
Charles Haddon Spurgeon

"A wedding anniversary is the celebration of love, trust, partnership, tolerance and tenacity. The order varies for any given year."
Paul Sweeney

29

Courage

The Guiding Principle in Every Choice We Make

As a writer and entrepreneur, I often struggle to do justice to certain topics. In trying to describe the kind of courage required to start and grow a great company, both words and analogies sometimes fail me.

Even so, I still believe entrepreneurs are some of the most courageous people I know. Notwithstanding the contributions of our men and women in the armed forces, police, fire and other emergency services, I view many entrepreneurs as real American heroes.

Simply knowing everyone is counting on you to exercise good judgment, creativity, tenacity, and strength day after day is a very heavy load to carry. It is equally difficult to stand against market pressures that push us to lie, cheat, steal, and take shortcuts in order to remain competitive. Courage is definitely required.

Recently, as I was turning the whole concept of courage over in my mind while driving to work, something happened that gave me a totally new perspective.

You see, on Monday morning as I came rolling down the highway at 65 mph (well, ok, it may have been a tad bit faster), I saw a large turtle attempting to cross the road. Just as I approached, he was walking right up to the middle of my lane. By the time I noticed him, there was no time to stop and nowhere else to go—so over him I went.

Now, before you get all emotional and start firing off angry emails using words like "turtle slayer" or "tortoise abuser," rest assured that no reptiles were injured in the making of this book. Quite to the contrary, my car passed clean over the little fellow and he even turned his tiny green head to stare at me as I drove away. Seems as though being low to the ground and having an aerodynamic shell is a real plus in this part of the world (too bad about all those tall armadillos we just can't seem to miss).

On the way home that night, I passed the same turtle, except now he was perched exactly on the middle white stripe with his head and appendages tucked neatly into his shell. It seems he had experienced all the excitement he wanted for one day. On Tuesday morning, he had made it completely across, under cover of darkness no doubt, and was safely making his way down the side of the highway. Good for him.

So what does a turtle crossing the highway have to do with courage?

Just imagine living in a world that is moving faster than you can even turn your head. Think about dealing with problems hundreds of times larger than you, speeding at you from all directions. Try to envision being on a path of discovery that ultimately leaves you trapped in the dead middle of problems and challenges you have never even considered. Now, stay calm, make a plan, and try not to get flattened as you work toward your goal.

In my humble estimation, turtles and entrepreneurs have a lot in common. And no, I am not talking about having a hard shell. Although it does help sometimes.

Both are required to use every tool, past experience and a large measure of good judgment if they wish to simply survive their surroundings. Both have to get used to thriving in a world filled with incomplete information, inadequate resources, and sometimes, just plain bad drivers. Oh, and a little bit of luck goes a long way too.

Growing Forward

With these things in mind, I encourage you to consider some of these examples of simple courage as you move through your work week. You may even want to recommit yourself to being a leader who stands up right in the middle of things that aren't working, knowing full well that others may blame you for their own problems. If you do, good for you!

I call that turtle courage, my friend!

Treasure This

"So do not fear, for I am with you; do not be dismayed, for I am your God. I will strengthen you and help you; I will uphold you with my righteous right hand."
Isaiah 41:10, NIV

"Never bend your head. Always hold it high. Look the world straight in the eye."
Helen Keller

"It is not the critic who counts, not the man who points out how the strong man stumbled, or where the doer of deeds could have done better. The credit belongs to the man who is actually in the arena, whose face is marred by dust and sweat and blood, who strives valiantly, who errs and comes short again and again, who knows the great enthusiasms, the great devotions, and spends himself in a worthy cause, who at best knows achievement and who at the worst if he fails at least fails while daring greatly, so that his place shall never be with those cold and timid souls who know neither victory nor defeat."
Theodore Roosevelt
From a speech given in Paris at the Sorbonne in 1910

30

Distractions

Casting Them Off to Lighten Our Load

It's 10:30 on a Wednesday morning, and I am beginning to write this new chapter for my book. Right on time—how about that?!

Whoops. Glancing at my calendar, I just noticed I was supposed to start on this at 10:30 a.m. all right, but on Monday. I wonder where the last 48 hours went?

Does this ever happen to you?

It seems to me that distractions increase in direct proportion to the number of people we interact with, projects we take on, and expertise we gain in a given area. The best example that comes to mind is what happens at a tractor pull.

For those of you who don't get out into the country much, a tractor pull is a spectator event (particularly popular in the south) where highly modified tractors compete to determine which one can pull the heaviest weight. The weight comes in the form of a towing sled that has a moving load of several tons that shifts forward as the tractor pulls it down the track. As the load moves forward, the weight increases tremendously until it forces the tractor to a stop – sometimes even causing it to wheelie and then turn over. Pretty exciting stuff—especially if you don't have cable TV at home.

As leaders, distractions are like the weighted load on a tractor. The farther we go, the heavier it gets until it either stops us or turns us over. Sounds like it's time to lighten up, but how?

Here are some fast and easy ways to cut down on the *drag* that distractions create in your life:

- Set aside an hour every week to look back on what you were able to accomplish during the last seven days.
- Start a list of recurring distractions—phone calls, deadlines, employee crises, etc.
- Look for common causes for the distractions you have listed and determine ways to make dealing with those causes more proactive and routine. Examples:
  » Set aside a portion of each morning and afternoon to return calls, emails, bids, and proposals.
  » Block out several hours each week to plan next week's activities.
  » Teach your employees to group their questions, ideas, and issues and then bring them to you in writing or email so that together you can take action on them all at once.
  » Teach your employees to bring answers to their own questions—before you meet with them. That way, they will have thought it through already and take up less of your time.
  » Set limits on when you will take outside calls and instruct your staff to get the full name, title, company, and purpose of every call coming to you.

» Stay home! If you are working against a project deadline and you want to minimize distractions, don't come into the office. Work from home until you are finished.

» Value your own time—decide what your time is worth and do not "sell it cheap" just because someone wants some of it.

• Enlist your entire company in the process. Remember, if it's distracting to you it's probably distracting your managers and employees. Teach your people how to manage their time to leverage the high-value work and let go of the low-value/low-return activities.

• Routinely (at least twice per year) sit down as a group and map out the changes in customers, vendors, projects, revenues, etc. that are now impacting how everyone manages their time. Since a company is a living thing, time requirements change rapidly. Effectiveness depends on everyone recognizing and reacting to these changes in cost-effective ways.

The old saying "time is money" succinctly expresses the fact that we perpetually trade our only real asset (our time) for the common currency of exchange (money). Sometimes, however, we get so busy that we begin to settle for less and less in exchange for our time.

Never exchange high-value work for low-value returns!

Growing Forward

As you move through this week, I encourage you to look at your schedule (and then your staff's schedules) with a critical eye toward the activities and issues that are weighing on everyone's time and slowing down your operation. Then, start incorporating some of these ideas into your daily experience. You will be surprised at how heavy your sled has become. Feel free to lighten the load!

Treasure This

"Therefore, since we also have such a great cloud of witnesses surrounding us, let's rid ourselves of every obstacle and the sin which so easily entangles us, and let's run with endurance the race that is set before us, looking only at Jesus, the [a]originator and perfecter of the faith, who for the joy set before Him endured the cross, despising the shame, and has sat down at the right hand of the throne of God."
Hebrews 12:1-2, NIV

"One way to boost our willpower and focus is to manage our distractions instead of letting them manage us."
Daniel Goleman

"Please do not confuse my visibility with my availability."
Pat Higgins

31

Resilience

Enhancing Our Lives From Lessons Learned

Have you ever thought to yourself: "It just can't get any worse than this"?

If you have been on this planet for any significant period of time, you already know the truth about how real life works, so your next thought may be, "Sure it can—and it probably will!"

As a matter of fact, this is the reason we have such popular old sayings as:

"Murphy's Law"
"It's always darkest before the dawn"
"Sometimes you just can't catch a break"
"My momma told me there would be days like this"
"Sometimes you eat the bear and sometimes the bear eats you"

Some enterprising musicians have even turned this "bad to worse" phenomenon into an art form we affectionately call Country music.

Here are some of the more memorable titles:

"I was drunk the day my momma got out of prison"
"I'm just a bug on the windshield of life"
"I want a beer as cold as my ex-wife's heart"
"How can I miss you if you won't go away?"
"Thank God and Greyhound she's gone"
"You can't have your Kate and Edith too"

Before we can understand how to live a resilient life, I believe that we must confront certain realities that affect us all:

- Life is not fair, so get used to it.

- Sometimes we get what we deserve – other times we don't (and often that's a *good* thing).

- People will disappoint us, and we will often disappoint others and especially ourselves.

- It is not that hard to get into more trouble than we can get out of.

- The easy way of doing things is seldom the right way.

- There are many benefits to living a life dedicated to serving others before ourselves.

- Good will ultimately win out over evil.

- We only get one chance at this life and we should try to make the most of it.

Living a resilient life is a choice. It has a lot to do with understanding that while things don't always go our way, we can still move ahead step by step. Even though we cannot control everything that happens to us, we do get to choose how we respond and the attitude we have in the midst of the struggles.

As a leader, you already know that many people are watching how you respond to adversity. Your people will pattern much of their behavior and attitude after yours when faced with their own obstacles.

Here are some ways that you can help them become more resilient in response to life's little calamities:

- Be transparent – people relate and respond to leaders who are open about their flaws and mistakes. They want to know that excellence is the goal rather than perfection.

- Be persistent – model the process of getting up and dusting yourself off after encountering a setback. Everyone falls; it is the ones who get up again that make a difference in our world.

- Be proactive – find new and more effective ways to get the old jobs done. Many future problems can be avoided if we don't wait until things break to improve them.

- Be hands-on – everyone appreciates a leader who chooses to learn about problems and struggles by getting their hands dirty with the rest of the troops. Respect is born in the trenches.

- Be forgiving – start with yourself and then your people while learning to move past the "blame game" and on to the "lessons learned" part of the forgiveness process. Offenses that go unresolved and unforgiven become a heavy burden on the entire organization.

- Be a servant – choose to be the last in line for everything. Make it a point to ensure that your people have everything they need to do their jobs before you go looking for ways to make yours easier.

Growing Forward

Hard times and struggles in life are a sure thing, just like death and taxes. Look ahead to the coming week and make a list of ways you can model *resilience* for your people in the midst of the struggles you are going through.

Remember: "Winners never quit—and quitters never win!"

Treasure This

"No temptation has taken you except what is common to man. God is faithful, who will not allow you to be tempted above what you are able, but will with the temptation also make the way of escape, that you may be able to endure it."
1 Corinthians 10:13, NASB

"Life is not a matter of holding good cards, but of playing a poor hand well."
Robert Louis Stevenson

"Those who dare, win."
Motto of the British Special Air Services

32

Pain

Leading Through It, Learning From It

Okay folks, it's time to put your tough shirts on.

The subject is "How do I lead my company while I am going through serious (maybe even life-threatening) pain?" I have experienced this firsthand for almost a decade, so I won't waste your time or mine dancing around the subject. Here is how I see it.

In 1995, I was hit by a personal watercraft and suffered a lot of damage to my right hip and lower back. This accident started a long struggle through chronic back and leg pain. It has affected every part of my life, especially my family and business relationships. For a long time, I had to simply drop off "the grid" while I worked with doctors, physical therapists, and pain management specialists to learn how to handle the pain while still maintaining a sound mind. With the help of these dedicated professionals and the love and support of my family, friends, church, and employees I was able to fight my way back to about 65 percent of my previous effectiveness.

In 2005, I underwent a new procedure called total disc replacement, and since then, I have been able to do just about everything with only a medium amount of pain. I believe where I am today is the direct result of the consistent prayers and support of the people around me.

What about you?

Are you running a company while fighting cancer? Are you trying to grow your business while taking your mom or dad to dialysis? Has your son or daughter been diagnosed with a life-threatening illness? Was life rolling along fine until your body was crushed by a drunken driver running a red light?

Here is what I have learned about chronic pain and illness:
- It is not a question of *if* but rather of *when* we will have to deal with it.
- It has a way of stopping everything in our lives and dominating our minds.
- It affects everything and will crush our spirit if we let it.
- It makes us want to hide from others who are healthy.
- It can feel like the loneliest place on earth.
- It often seems totally unfair, and we usually don't see it coming.
- It seems the only people who really understand it are the ones who are going through it themselves.
- It never lets up or gives us a break; it is a 24/7 kind of thing.
- It is often as or more painful for our loved ones than for us.
- It takes away who we are and makes us into someone we don't want to be.

But, the most important thing I have learned about chronic pain and illness is this:

It can be overcome, and we can take back our lives!

Here is how:

- Let out your frustrations: Throw a pity party and get it out of your system. Call up your closest friends and family (at least one person), sit them down and spell it out for them, including how you really feel about it, especially your feelings of fear and loss. Now, at least everyone is on the same page and together you can make some plans.

- Line up your resources: Treatments, recovery periods and pain meds should all be factored into a schedule to help you manage your pain and treatment while having the least impact on your business. Be realistic about how treatments and medication will affect your mood and judgment. Your people are counting on you to be as good as you can be while going through this.

- Lean on your friends, family and advisors: Select a person in each area of your life to keep an eye on you. Give your spouse permission to monitor your results. Task a close friend with helping you stay engaged at a minimal level with church and social interactions. Ask senior managers or lead employees to give feedback on how they perceive your leadership and business dealings.

- Look to the future: Living in chronic pain or illness is like one very long night with no sunrise in sight. To win this battle, we have to believe there is a glorious sunrise in our future. Often this belief is all that carries us from one day to the next. We are each responsible for our own attitudes. If we think things will only get worse, it is almost a sure thing that they will. Guard against this. Stay positive. The impossible cure just might happen for you – it did for me!

- Live in an attitude of gratitude: Focusing on what you have lost is a normal response, but it won't help you heal. Remember, the point of all this is to improve your situation by what you can control. Gratitude is good medicine.

- Lead with transparency: I subscribe to the notion that adversity does not build character; it simply reveals it. Your pain and incapacity will reveal many things to your people, and some won't be very pretty. Why not take this opportunity to become a more genuine leader? Why not bring your key people closer to you and delegate more responsibilities to them? Not only will this lighten your load and hasten your healing; it will also boost their sense of partnership with you. Sharing control builds trust and lessens everyone's anxiety.

- Learn to laugh more: Like gratitude, laughter is great medicine. We live in a funny world, and laughing releases a lot of the good chemicals our bodies need to heal. There comes a point when getting poked by yet another needle or hanging upside down in a skimpy hospital gown just seems absurd enough to chuckle about. Been there, done that.

- Live your life with purpose: Pain and illness steal our life before it kills us. Don't let it! Choose to live your life on your own terms. Prioritize how you live your life and guard against wasting precious time feeling sorry for yourself. Make the most of what you have to work with today and live your life like you mean it!

Well, I told you to put your tough shirt on, and by now I'll bet you are glad you did. There are not many things that I am an expert on, but when it comes to pain, I believe I am a world-class authority!

Enduring pain is not a choice—overcoming it with purpose is!

Growing Forward

Take some time away this week and jot down your priorities for living your life and running your business when pain becomes your companion. Then start living out those priorities now. The sooner you take real control of your situation in the good times, the more likely you will be successful in the hard times. Remember, there are people praying and hoping for you right now – there will be even more when things get tough, many you won't even know about!

Treasure This

"And God shall wipe away all tears from their eyes; and there shall be no more death, neither sorrow, nor crying, neither shall there be any more pain: for the former things are passed away."
Revelations 21:4, KJV

"It is easier to find men who will volunteer to die, than to find those who are willing to endure pain with patience."
Julius Caesar

"Pain is temporary. It may last a minute, or an hour, or a day, or a year, but eventually it will subside and something else will take its place. If I quit, however, it lasts forever."
Lance Armstrong

33

Direction

Finding Our Way Forward

If you don't know where you are going, any path will do.

And so it is with our lives.

How often do we as leaders find ourselves in crisis, not knowing where to go and what to do next? At times like these, I often think back to the little wind-up car I once had that would bump into the wall, stop, and then turn around and go in the opposite direction— until it hit another wall. While this was very entertaining to me as a child, these days, running my company into the wall is absolutely no fun at all!

So, how do we find our way when confronted with life altering choices?

In 1991, shortly after the beginning of the first Gulf War, my Dad died. I missed him on so many levels. He had been my lifelong mentor, confidant, advocate, and friend. Dad was not just a wonderful father and husband; he was also a real leader who lived out what he believed.

As a career soldier (Command Sergeant Major) he had experienced two wars as a front-line warrior. He had also spent over 30 years training other soldiers how to survive and effectively function in the midst of unimaginable chaos. He spent his days surrounded by artillery pieces, weapons, and war plans; but when he came home, he took off the uniform and became simply Dad.

Shortly after his passing, I began thinking about the many ways Dad had invested his life to positively change the life direction of many young soldiers. It did not take long before I was asking myself questions like, "Well, Tony, you are 36 years old. Your life is about half over, and what have you done to make the world better?" While I had done a good job as a husband, father and overall provider, I knew I was capable of much more, so I decided to change directions.

My first baby step was to enroll in a nine-day Outward Bound course that took place in the Blue Ridge Mountains of North Carolina. Activities including mountain hiking, rock climbing, and a high ropes course were downright terrifying to me. And did I mention I am afraid of heights? But off I went.

Even though I had prepared myself physically for the challenges of the course, I had no way of knowing what a mental and spiritual life-changer it would be. The single issue that made this time so memorable for me was the *rain*.

It rained every day, all day and all night. I had never been so wet for so long in all of my life. There is just something about being cold and wet for days at a time that sucks the life right out of a person, and so it was for us. Here were twelve strong, focused individuals who had come together to reaffirm their life purposes in the great outdoors— reduced to soggy, defeated, whining children in just a few short days.

Fortunately for all of us, things were about to change!

On the morning of our fifth day out, our leader called a meeting and told us we had a choice to make. "Give in to the elements and let them defeat you, or get it together, make a plan, and make it work," she said. For reasons I still don't completely understand (but will always be grateful for), several of us decided we'd had enough whining and moaning and wanted to take charge of our collective miserable circumstances. From that point until the end of the trip, attitudes, relationships, and the overall reality of being stuck out there improved dramatically.

On the last night of our time up in the mountains, we sat around in a circle (no campfires here—still too wet—just a little alcohol stove for boiling water) and entered into a time-honored Outward Bound tradition, "The Pinning Ceremony."

Our instructor opened up a small bag and laid 12 Outward Bound lapel pins on the ground. She told us to each take one, hold it in our hands and think about the person in the group who had taught us the most significant lessons during our time together. Soon after, one by one, people began moving around the circle, pinning one another and sharing with the group what that person had meant to them during our adventure.

When everyone had received their pins, our instructor slowly looked around the circle and said, "We have all now traveled this trail together. Soon you will need to travel a new trail of your own making. What do you want your trail to look like?" One by one each team member described the trail that they hoped would mark the rest of their lives.

When the time came for me to describe the trail I hoped to travel in the future, I could hardly believe my own ears. I said, "Make my trail steep and muddy. Throw in some rocks and boulders just to keep things interesting. When I have conquered the trail, I will know that my life was worth living."

While I probably should have chosen something a little less strenuous, I am not sure that I would change a thing. God, my family, friends, employees, customers, doctors, nurses and dozens of others have helped me grow and overcome at every turn and every obstruction on my trail from that day to this one.

We will all go down a trail in life. Isn't it better to choose our own than to have it chosen for us?

Whatever place you presently find yourself, I encourage you to think critically about where you want to end up.

You can be certain no one else will understand where you want your life's trail to lead if you don't.

Growing Forward

Before we can effectively lead others, we must know where we want to go and how we want to make the journey. Today would be a great day to start considering your new direction. Start by asking, "Is the path I am presently on taking me where I want to end up?" If the answer is anything but a resounding YES, start making your plans to follow a new trail – the trail your heart yearns to follow.

Treasure This

"Where there is no guidance the people fall, But in an abundance of counselors there is victory."
Proverbs 11:14, NASB

"I find the great thing in this world is not so much where we stand, as in what direction we are moving; to reach the port of Heaven, we must sail sometimes with the wind and sometimes against it, but we must sail, and not drift, nor lie at anchor."
Oliver Wendell Holmes

"Leaders establish the vision for the future and set the strategy for getting there; they cause change. They motivate and inspire others to go in the right direction and they, along with everyone else, sacrifice to get there."
John Kotter

34

Burnout

───────────── // ─────────────

Learning to recognize our limits

So there we were at last: Seattle in the fall. What a beautiful place to vacation.

My wife Jane and I had finally arrived at our destination a mere 18 months from the time we started. No, it does not take that long to fly from North Texas to Washington State. But it does take that long to handle all the tasks of selling a company and securing a serious case of executive burnout in the process.

As we were seated at a table for two at Champagne, a lovely French restaurant just across the street from the famous Pikes Place Market on the Seattle waterfront, I caught a glimpse of a dog nestled under the table next to us. In Seattle, people take their dogs with them into restaurants like folks in other cities take their children. Consequently, I didn't consider seeing the dog in such an upscale establishment all that unusual.

After we ordered our lunch, I overheard one of the two ladies sitting next to us talking about her dog, saying what a wonderful friend and companion he was to her. I could only see the dog's head over the top of the table, but I did notice that like my own Samson and Goliath, her hound was a yellow Labrador retriever. Being a proud dog owner, I whipped out my iPhone and held up a photo of my dogs for her to see. Then I said, "Excuse me Ma'am, I couldn't help noticing what a handsome yellow Lab you have there. We also have a couple of yellow Labs; aren't they great dogs?"

Hearing my voice, the lady turned her head in my direction, smiled, and said, "Sir, I'm sorry, I'm blind—but I am sure that your dogs are just as handsome as mine!"

The next few seconds seemed to last for hours. My first reaction was to look more closely at the lady's face. Sure enough, her eyes were wide open, but they didn't respond to her environment. Next, I ducked my head under the table to discover that her dog was indeed wearing a service harness for his master to hold on to. Finally, I looked directly across the table at Jane, just in time to see her blowing red wine out of her nose. She was fighting back tears of tortured, silent laughter at my stupendous social blunder.

For the next day and a half, each time a dog came into sight, Jane would break into spontaneous laughter recalling the incident. Eventually, I did too. We spent hours talking about how under normal circumstances, I would have picked up on the signs that the dog was a service animal and that his master was blind. The reason I had missed all of those signs was simple—I was too burned out and too fried to notice the details people usually pick up on without thinking about it.

Burnout occurs when we are required to remain too focused for too long. Without time away from the burdens of responsibility that define being a parent, spouse, business owner or leader, our ability to accurately assess facts and render high-quality judgments becomes severely limited. Not only do we become erratic in our thinking and judgment, but we can also become unpredictable and annoying in our behavior. Those who look to us for leadership and inspiration rapidly become frustrated with our lack of focus and direction.

In my experience, entrepreneurs and leaders are often the last people to make the time to take proper care of themselves. This and the natural aggressiveness required to run a company make them primary candidates for serious burnout. Ultimately, they pay a high price for denying themselves the opportunity to get away and recharge.
Here are some of the problems that can occur when leaders fail to recognize they need a break:

- Higher employee turnover—No one likes to work for a grump. Burnout makes us difficult to deal with and pushes people away from us. Sometimes, it even makes us want to quit!

- Lost opportunities—Burned-out leaders miss the subtle signs that point to new opportunities. It does not take long until these lost opportunities add up to seriously hurt the enterprise.

- Personal dissatisfaction—Most of us know when we are doing our best work. The longer we allow burnout to prevent us from being our best, the more likely it is we will become dissatisfied with our own performance.

- Competitive disadvantage—As a visionary leader we are the engine that drives the company forward. A healthy balance is critical to preventing the company from becoming disadvantaged in the competitive marketplace.

On the flip side, there are advantages to routinely making time to refresh and recharge ourselves, including:

- Regaining perspective—As we relax, our brains regain the ability to focus and effectively interpret and analyze information.

- Refreshing our sense of humor—It's good to laugh, especially at ourselves. Time away allows us to stop taking ourselves so seriously all the time.

- Reestablishing relationships—As busy entrepreneurs, taking time away to just be ourselves gives us the chance to strengthen life-long bonds with the folks who are the most important to us.

- Rediscovering our passions—To live balanced and fulfilling lives we must live out our passions while building significant lives for ourselves and families.

Earlier, I mentioned that Jane stopped laughing at my blunder with the blind lady and her dog a day and a half into our vacation.

The reason?

On our second day in Seattle we decided to participate in a local Oktoberfest celebration. After a couple of hours (and four samples of the local ale) she decided that it was time to visit the local ladies room. We walked through the crowd until we saw a row of bright blue plastic porta-potties in a nearby clearing. I stood by the bratwurst stand while Jane proceeded to go door to door searching for an unoccupied outhouse. After finding no success with the first 10 doors she tried, she turned to look over at me only to discover that she had ignored about 150 fellow celebrants who were patiently waiting (with seriously distressed bladders) for their turn to relieve themselves. While no one called out to her, the pained expressions on their faces said it all.

Now it was my turn to choke on a half-swallowed bratwurst as Jane made her way in morbid disgrace to the back of the privy queue.

I guess being burned out can be contagious!

Growing Forward

Burnout is such a common condition among high-performing entrepreneurs that we often joke about it. But after the laughter dies down we have to face the serious reality that burnout severely and negatively affects us in ways we don't even comprehend.

Take some time this week to consider how long it has been since you really had a break to get away and refresh yourself and your family. Then, set a date, carve it in stone on your calendar and start planning a retreat, vacation, sabbatical or secret getaway that will ensure that the very best you returns renewed and refreshed.

Treasure This

"Come to Me, all [a]who are weary and burdened, and I will give you rest."
Matthew 11:28, NASB

"When weariness, discouragement, over-commitment, and insecurity meet in front of our house, burnout is just around the corner."
Tony Ford

"It is our best work that God wants, not the dregs of our exhaustion. I think he must prefer quality to quantity."
George MacDonald

35

Struggle

////

Our Common Condition Requires
Uncommon Courage

February 23, 2003 found me sitting in yet another doctor's office waiting to be poked, prodded, pierced or medicated for my chronic back pain. Today there would be a brief examination and then another bi-weekly routine of 16 injections to help my wounded back heal. In the eight years since getting run over by a personal watercraft, I had sunk to a very low point of depression. The struggle continued.

As I looked around the dreary, cheaply furnished waiting room I was overwhelmed by the feeling that I simply did not belong there. The room was stuffy, poorly lit, and crammed full of broken people in all stages of pain and debilitation. These folks were not like me. They did not look like me. They did not talk like me. They smelled of defeat and resignation.

In short, these people had just given up on life.

Lord, please help me, I prayed. *I'm trapped in a room with **those** people.*

You know who I am talking about. You see them all over the place: in airports and hospitals, sidewalks and laundromats, alleyways and bus stops. Those unfortunate people who know the back of life's hand across their faces. Sick, tired, broken people who have suffered through multiple surgeries, been ravaged by diseases or are simply too depressed to respond to even the best things life offers. They have given up on themselves and given in to despair and despondency.

I had seen these sick, pitiful, broken people all of my life. It was not possible that I had become one of them—or was it?

As we journey through life, not only is it possible to become one of *those people* – it is almost inevitable. At some point in our lives we will come face to face with a struggle that saps our strength and wipes out our resources. It may be cancer or mental illness or the death of a loved one or loss of our business or… I'm sure you can fill in your own blank.

Along with the struggle will come many choices. The first will be whether or not we acknowledge the truth of our circumstances. The truth says "*I AM one of those people*"! You see we are all one of those people—common strugglers on a common journey through life.

As an entrepreneur, others look to us for answers and expect us to overcome obstacles at every turn. But when the day comes that our answers fall short and the obstacles overwhelm us, it is critical to recognize the indispensable value of seeking the help of others to struggle through to new understandings.

The lessons I have learned from the common struggles, from being one of *those people*, have illuminated my leadership by energizing my empathy. I now know it is empathy and understanding that empowers my ability to support the dreams of others. It is the "soft side" of entrepreneurship.

I want to live the balance of my life as a transparent example of how the grace of God—often demonstrated through helpful, caring people—has carried me when I could not move forward in my own strength.

When we allow humbling circumstances to soften our hearts instead of hardening them, we become more effective entrepreneurs and leaders; but maybe more importantly, we allow the truth of our own frailty to teach us what, and *who*, to value.

What doesn't kill us does make us stronger
- but only if we don't give up!

Growing Forward

As you go through your world this week, look around for *those people* (they won't be hard to find). Lend them a hand in their struggle – because struggle is our common condition.

Treasure This

"For our struggle is not against flesh and blood, but against the rulers, against the powers, against the world forces of this darkness, against the spiritual forces of wickedness in the heavenly places."
Ephesians 6:12, NASB

"Opportunity follows struggle. It follows effort. It follows hard work. It doesn't come before."
Shelby Steele

"By compassion we make others' misery our own, and so, by relieving them, we relieve ourselves also."
Thomas Browne, Sr.

SECTION FIVE

CHARACTER

36

Provision

///

Trusting God for Our Needs

The winter of 1981 found me selling commercial light bulbs door to door as I struggled to figure out what God wanted me to do with my life. I had just left the Seminary after two and a half years of work and study, only to find myself back on the street trying to make a living. It took me that long to figure out that I did not have a "Pastor's Heart". Jane was still working for IBM (which was why we weren't starving), and we lived in a broken-down rent house that required perpetual maintenance just to remain inhabitable.

I was frustrated, confused, angry, and very impatient to get on with my life.

Being young and dumb, I did not yet understand that at the heart of every successful sale was the need to establish a trusting relationship with the customer. All I wanted to do was sell everyone I called as many light bulbs as they would take without regard to what they really needed for their business to benefit. My lack of sales was a direct reflection of my own ignorance of the sales process and my lack of desire to build strong customer relationships. My motives were wrong, my approach was poor, and my attitude was getting worse with every call I made. Besides those things, I was in great shape.

The first week of my third month on the job passed without a single sale. I was making the sales calls, showing the products, even asking the right questions, yet nothing was happening.

I got into my old Mazda 626 (with 127,000 miles on it) and headed for home. Along the way, I passed by a seafood restaurant that had that old fish and tackle shop look about it. You know — rusty tin roof, bait buckets, oars, and life preservers hanging from spider web-covered fish nets. "Surely," I thought, "These guys don't need any light bulbs." But, having nothing to lose, I decided to stop there anyway and make one last pitch for the week.

When I walked in, there was an old man sitting at the end of the bar shuffling through some paperwork. I introduced myself, and he said that he was the owner. I ordered a Coke from the bartender, and the owner and I started talking restaurant shop talk. Over an hour passed, and the subject of light bulbs never even came up. I really liked this guy, and apparently he liked me.

Finally, the man asked me what I did for a living. I told him that I sold commercial lighting products. He said he had some lighting issues that I might be able to help him with. For the next hour, we toured his restaurant, and I pointed out different ways he could use colored and high-intensity lighting to make his kitchen, salad bar, and dining rooms really come to life. When we sat back down, he ordered over $3,000 worth of new light bulbs. That was 150% of my weekly goal!

When the next Monday came, I was fired up and ready to whip the world. Just like the week before, I found myself driving back from Dallas to Fort Worth at 4:00 on Friday afternoon with zero sales to show for my efforts.

I noticed an old factory building that seemed to have a lot of cars parked around it. I circled back, went inside, and found out that the new owner was re-working the interior to make custom draperies. After a few minutes, I met the owner and asked him to show me around with an eye toward making some recommendations for how to best light the work areas. One thing led to another, and within two hours, I had made a $4,200 sale. I simply could not believe my luck!

On the way home, I thought about how strange it was that I would make my weekly sales goal in a single sale on Friday afternoon two weeks in a row. *Maybe this isn't luck*, the thought struck me. *Maybe it is God's provision*. Right then, driving down I-35, I said a little prayer of thanksgiving to God. After sharing the story with Jane, she, too, pointed out how God was looking out for us and providing more than we even needed. Now God had my attention.

Monday morning of the third week came, and I started trying different sales approaches. I called on new types of businesses. I even tried a few government offices. By 3:00 pm on Friday, the results were the same as before. Still no sales.

With the last two weeks' events still fresh in my mind, I prayed and asked God what he was trying to teach me. Turning off of Camp Bowie Blvd. onto University Drive, I saw a sign in the window of a strip shopping center that read *Coming Soon—Flash Foto*. I walked inside to find the empty shell of a retail store with a telephone number painted on the wall in 6" high letters. I called the number, and the owner answered after the first ring. We began discussing the new store he was building. Soon, he invited me over to his office a few blocks away, and off I went.

By the time our two-hour-long conversation was over, he had purchased $3,200 worth of color-corrected lighting for his new one-hour-photo finishing store. He also offered me a job to become his new General Manager in charge of growing the first chain of one-hour photo finishing stores in North Texas. I accepted his offer, and we went on to build a chain of eight retail stores and a commercial processing lab with over $3 million in sales in just 18 months. Flash Foto became the springboard that launched my entrepreneurial career!

When I got home that night, Jane and I sat on the couch and recounted the events of the last three weeks.

In that time, God had:
- Demonstrated his total provision for us three times in the very same way
- Opened a new door of opportunity to use my training and skills
- Taught me the value of seeking to serve the needs of other people, not just myself
- Given us insight into the futility of only relying on our own efforts to succeed
- Inspired us to seek after and ask for opportunities in faith
- Proved we could wait patiently for his perfect timing to fulfill our needs
- Shown we could trust him with the desires of our hearts

In the years to come, I would remember those events as the first step in what would become a series of servant-led businesses.

In the 30-plus years since these doors were opened to us, Jane and I have had a front-row seat to witness how God is totally dependable in making provision for his people. We have started and managed businesses that employed hundreds of people. Our products and services have enhanced the lives of thousands of customers across the country and around the world. Yet, through it all, we have not felt overly stressed about having to have all the answers. Our job has been to be good stewards of the people and resources God has placed in our care. This process has strengthened our faith, stretched our emotional and spiritual muscles, and found us serving the needs of many wonderful folks.

This is not to say we have not experienced pain, setbacks, disappointments, and heartaches. It is to say that in every case, at the perfect time, God has provided just the right help in the right amounts so we could overcome the circumstances of life.

It is for these reasons we have declared, "Choose this day whom you will serve. As for me and my house, we will serve the Lord" (Joshua 24:15) as our cornerstone because it represents how we feel about trusting God for our provisions.

Let's face it: life is hard and very unfair at times. And while this often seems to surprise us, it never surprises God. With this in mind, our choices seem pretty simple:

A) Depend on our own resources and wisdom to overcome the world and its problems

or

B) Depend on the One who created the world to support us as we face its challenges by faith.

Growing Forward

As a leader, your days are filled with problems to solve and people who are unhappy. You know firsthand how hard it is to bear up under the pressures of running a business. I invite you to take some time this week to look back over your life; specifically, try to identify the instances where God intervened to turn around what at that moment seemed to be a hopeless situation.

You may be surprised at how often God has been your real provision all along!

Treasure This

"Trust in the Lord with all your heart and do not lean on your own understanding. In all your ways acknowledge Him, and He will make your paths straight."
Proverbs 3:5-6, NASB

"When God gives you vision, He will also give you provision."
Ronnie L Williams

"But my God shall supply all your need according to his riches in glory by Christ Jesus."
Paul the Apostle

37

Character

The Gift You Give Yourself

"Going through hard times doesn't build character, it simply reveals it."

The idea behind this old saying is that our true character becomes much more apparent when we are faced with difficult circumstances. I have found that true in my own life. It seems that we are all pretty accomplished actors when it comes to adapting to our environment and the roles we are expected to play. For eight to 10 hours each day, we quite easily go through the motions of being "the boss." But what happens when things start to fall apart? What character traits do our employees witness, then?

Many years ago, I was chosen to participate in a trade delegation trip to represent the U.S. in Tokyo, Japan. More than 20 other nations were represented as we traveled together around the city, touring the major manufacturers there. On the second night of the two-week trip, I was in a hotel elevator going up to my room for the night when it stopped, and a young lady from the Canada delegation got on. When the doors closed, she turned to me and said, "You have no idea how much I want to have a man in my bed tonight!" I thought I had heard her wrong, so like a dummy, I asked her what she had just said. She repeated herself (a little slower this time to make sure I got the message) and then shot me her best "Come and get me" grin.

For some guys, being trapped in an elevator 8,000 miles away from home with an attractive woman would seem like a dream come true. For me, it was a nightmare. Since nothing like this had ever happened to me, I decided to simply listen to my inner voice and act accordingly. I looked the woman in the eye and said, "Well, best of luck with that—but it won't be me." Then, just as she was about to object, the elevator doors opened on my floor, and I pushed my way past her.

When I got to my room (and my heart stopped racing), I had to take a few minutes to think about what had just happened and how I had responded. Once I had it all clear in my mind, I called my wife, Jane, and shared the entire episode with her. While she was shocked, she seemed to understand the dynamics of the situation better than I did and talked me through the whole "she is a single girl out for a wild time in Japan" concept. Needless to say, I kept my distance from that lady for the balance of the trip.

Now, when I mention I listened to my inner voice, I am talking about the combination of experiences and commitments that determine who I am as a person. This defines my true character and is important for a variety of reasons we would do well to understand:

- Character is a self-defining gift—When no one else is watching, character is the gift that we give ourselves in order to define who we are no matter what the circumstances or surroundings may be. We carry it around with us, and it helps protect us in situations that we can't predict or control.

- Character is an obligation to those we love–When our loved ones are not around to represent themselves and their values, character is what keeps us true to them. It says, "I act this way because I have made promises to people I love."

• Character is a shining light to others—When confronted with problems or behaviors we know are not right, our character confronts them and models another way to go. Sometimes it will be the first and only time the other person sees what they are doing is unacceptable.

• Character is a refuge—When others around us choose to "Go along to get along," it is our character that will protect us from participating in their duplicity. Organizations filled with yes people rapidly degenerate into mind-numbing cultures where creativity and imagination have no chance for survival.

• Character keeps us honest—It does not take long for wrong behaviors and attitudes in our lives to connect our character with our conscience and make a call to our brain that yells, "You are going the wrong way! Turn around!"

• Character is our teacher—As we get older, we seldom remember lessons learned from our successes. Rather, it is our great failures that tend to stick in our minds. Often my greatest failures started out as failures of character that soon blossomed into failures in judgment. I have learned a lot from looking back on these situations.

• Character is nonnegotiable—Most of us know the difference between right and wrong. If our character is available to be sold to the highest bidder, it is relatively worthless.

If our character is solid and nonnegotiable, it is more valuable than gold!

Growing Forward

Take some time this week to think back on times when your character has been tested or questioned. How did you respond? Life is full of second chances. Start deciding today how you will respond to life's challenges in the future. Becoming a person of character is a life journey—make yours a great one!

Treasure This

"But above all, my brothers and sisters, do not swear, either by heaven or by earth or with any other oath; but your yes is to be yes, and your no, no, so that you do not fall under judgment."
James 5:12, NASB

"Be more concerned with your character than your reputation, because your character is what you really are, while your reputation is merely what others think you are."
John Wooden

"Character cannot be developed in ease and quiet. Only through experience of trial and suffering can the soul be strengthened, vision cleared, ambition inspired, and success achieved."
Helen Keller

38

Humility

Growing With the Help of Others

Several years ago I came face to face with one of my many shortcomings—a tendency to talk when I should be listening.

A project partner and I were meeting with a potential investor at a very nice restaurant in downtown Fort Worth, Texas. My partner and I had agreed that we would spend the first 30 minutes of the meeting getting to know more about our guest and his dreams for the future. Since we already knew he shared a similar vision for working with entrepreneurs, it was almost certain our new project would be of interest to him.

Everyone showed up, and we began with the normal small talk— weather, kids, hometowns, etc. Our guest began sharing some of his ideas and visions for the future, and things were going quite well, until somehow I lost my bearings and forgot what we were all there to accomplish.

At first, this took the form of my asking questions about some of the more irrelevant things he mentioned, wasting valuable time for everyone at the table. Next, I started telling some of my old "war stories," causing even more delays.

As I looked across the table, I could see that my project partner was simply staring down at the table with a very dejected expression on her face. I remember thinking, "I wonder what's wrong with her today?" Had I asked her, the answer would have been very short (but not too sweet). She would have said, "What's wrong is YOU, Tony! You have totally forgotten what we agreed to and you have hijacked our presentation."

And so I had—and so it went until it was time for everyone to leave.

Several days later, after being out of town for other business, I called her to get caught up. It was obvious from her tone, something was very wrong. She came right to the point and shared her view of how the meeting had gone (very poorly) and how I had basically sabotaged a wonderful opportunity for us to move the project forward.

After hearing her impressions of the meeting, I fully understood that I was, in fact, "guilty as charged." No excuses, no denials – this was my fault. AGAIN.

I say again because, like so many character issues in our lives, most are repeats from the past. For me, it takes real discipline to listen more and talk less. It takes even more to participate in an orderly presentation with other people. In this case, I had totally failed.

This situation may sound unpleasantly familiar to many of you. Many of us talk when we should be listening. But my point is not to focus on a single character issue. It is to heighten our awareness of the fact we often need others to redirect us away from unhelpful behaviors, and blind spots. Indeed, we need to be humbled in this way on a regular basis to prevent pride and natural abilities from making us arrogant and unaware of how our actions affect others.

When we put on the mantle of Leader, Entrepreneur, or simply Boss, we are signing up for a higher standard of self-awareness. With so many people watching what we do and say, we need all the help we can get from others to keep our attitudes and actions genuine.

Humility is the currency that pays our way back into new opportunities. It is our agreement to "own our own stuff" and admit when we are wrong. Most importantly, it is the glue that bonds us all together in a common and interdependent struggle - the struggle to be more today than we were yesterday and to forgive others as they forgive us.

Remember, if we don't humble ourselves —life will surely do it for us!

Growing Forward

Take a few minutes this week and think about some recurring character issues that have caused you problems in the past. Then, find a trusted friend, mentor or coach to discuss them with you. Humble yourself and ask them to hold you accountable for improving one or two as you continue to grow as a person and a leader.

Treasure This

"Therefore humble yourselves under the mighty hand of God, that He may exalt you at the proper time."
1 Peter 5:6, NASB

"Humility must always be the portion of any man who receives acclaim earned in the blood of his followers and the sacrifices of his friends."
Dwight David Eisenhower

"What makes humility so desirable is the marvelous thing it does to us; it creates in us a capacity for the closest possible intimacy with God."
Monica Baldwin

39

Life-Long Learning

No Longer a Luxury for Leaders

It's "Car Tune-Up Day" at the Ford House.

I really used to enjoy "Car Tune-Up Day," but not so much anymore. You see, for many years , I have had to take our cars to the dealer to get a tune-up instead of doing it in my workshop. Why? Because I no longer feel competent to do the job.

Somewhere back in the mid to late 1990s, auto manufacturers started putting shrouds and covers over most of the working parts of the car's engine. On my car, the entire engine is covered by a shroud that simply has the make of the car and the size of the engine marked in large chrome letters. This is a nice way for the manufacturer to get across the real message, which is: "Hey moron, you may be smart enough to buy this car—but you are not NEARLY smart enough to work on it. So stay out of the engine compartment!"

When I first noticed this trend, I have to say I was both taken aback and offended that the manufacturer thought so poorly of their customers and our mechanical abilities that they would go to so much trouble to protect these poor little engines from us. Back in the day, many of us could completely strip down an engine, transmission, and drivetrain and have it all put back together (with only a few parts left over) by the end of the weekend.

Today, as I try to take a more mature view of the situation, I see it for what it is. Automotive technology has simply advanced at a rate that is too rapid for us shade tree mechanics to keep up with it. The automakers are just trying to keep us from hurting the cars (and probably ourselves). I guess that's what we get for focusing our attention on other things like college, work, marriage, kids, bills, mortgages, etc.

The rapid growth of technology, information, and computerization has permeated almost every area of our lives—health care, education, government, business, finances, shopping, and the list goes on. How, then, are we as leaders going to ever keep pace with this explosion of knowledge and new ways of doing things?

Over the past 30 years, I have been involved in the creation of nine different organizations. In those early years, my greatest contributions came from being able to understand and problem-solve in a wide variety of disciplines. Back then, we were rewarded for being *Generalists*. These days I work hard to remain an expert in one or two areas while maintaining a well-informed working knowledge in several others.

Today, specialization in our chosen field is almost a given. As reams of information flow into our awareness from overseas, the internet, educational organizations, etc., it takes a dedicated plan of action to become and remain a lifelong learner.

Here are a few tips that can help us stay on top of our game:

- Identify the areas of work and leadership that most reward you mentally, spiritually, physically, and financially.

- Determine if your present situation is the best match for your expertise and interests

- If it is, make a list of what you still need to learn to master your craft—then go get the training needed to do it.

- If it is not, make a list of projects or jobs that would be a much better fit, and then put together a plan to get the training needed to pursue the new opportunity. Either way, get your mind right about the fact that "yesterday's skills just won't get the job done anymore."

- Examine your retirement goals and determine if "life on the golf course or in the bass boat" is for you. Retirement for many of us simply means moving into work we enjoy more and can do on our own timetable.

- Go to the library or bookstore and get some books and magazines on subjects you have always wondered about but never explored. You may find your next company or career is waiting for you there in the pages.

- Consider turning your hobby into a business—passion is a key ingredient in entrepreneurial success.

- Start viewing the concept of learning in a different way. Grown-ups realize learning is not about cramming for an exam, it is about equipping ourselves to get the most out of life and its opportunities.

With all of this in mind, I invite you to join me in getting over the feeling of inadequacy we get when we lift the hood of our cars. Now that I understand where the automakers are coming from, I am okay with it. Well, alright. It still hurts a little.

Growing Forward

Take some time this week and ask yourself, "What new things do I need to learn about professionally, personally, and just for the fun of it?" Then, enroll in a workshop, seminar or class to start you on your new road to lifelong learning!

Treasure This

"A wise man will hear and increase in learning, and a man of understanding will acquire wise counsel."
Proverbs 1:5, NASB

"Experience, that most brutal of teachers. But you learn; my God do you learn."
C.S. Lewis

"Being ignorant is not so much a shame as being unwilling to learn."
Benjamin Franklin

40

Gratitude and Stewardship

Paying It Forward

The first refrains of the "Tribute to God be the Glory" goes like this:

> *How can I say thanks for all the joys you have given me?*
> *Things so undeserved, yet you gave to prove your love for me*
> *The voices of a million angels could not express my gratitude*
> *All that I am or ever hope to be, I owe it all to thee*
> *To God be the Glory, To God be the Glory, To God be the Glory*
> *For the things he has done.*

I think these verses nail down the basic core of how gratitude is related to stewardship. Often our greatest gratitude is inexpressible and our best stewardship is grossly insufficient. Even so, many of us are on a mission to become the best stewards we can be.

For most of my life I had enjoyed good health, strong family relationships, caring mentors, abundant learning opportunities and enjoyable work. Along the way, I invested several years doing full time give-back work for nonprofits and foundations dedicated to supporting small business growth around the country. It was very gratifying work.

A boating accident when I was 40 launched my 10-year struggle with chronic back pain. During those years I was given many opportunities to pull alongside other entrepreneurs who needed ideas or encouragement. Often, we suffered, struggled and persevered together until the job was done.

Finally when I turned 50, through the miracle of modern joint replacement, I became free of my crippling pain and was able to work and travel again. This experience caused me to ask, "Now what?" How do I take everything I have been through, everything I have learned, all the wonderful folks who have helped me and give back in a way that says a proper thank you? The answer was simple—I can't. Just as composer Andre Crouch wrote in his 'Tribute To God be the Glory' knew, it is at best a rhetorical question. For me, it is in this place that my inexpressible gratitude must lead to the best stewardship I can offer.

My best stewardship happens when I pay it forward and is best expressed in an "attitude of gratitude" that serves the needs of others. Those of us who have been given more than we need (or deserve) have the opportunity to give back so that others who come after us will have something significant and substantial to build on.

Here are just some of the ways we can express our gratitude through our stewardship:

- Share our resources—If our goal is to get all we can, can all we get and sit on the can, then it is time for us to remember all the folks who helped us along the way, and then find ways to give to others. If we start making a list of those who helped us when we could not help ourselves, chances are it will be a long list. Remember, it's not about making a fortune; it's about making a difference!

- Choosing to invest our time, not just spend it—When we spend time watching TV, sports, or doing any activity that simply makes us zone out, time is lost. When we invest our time teaching, mentoring, tutoring or just being available to others, we can expect there to be a return on investment.

- Recognizing needs and addressing them—Sometimes needs go unmet simply because no one even recognizes them. As entrepreneurs, we are uniquely gifted at discovering opportunities and building on them. Why not use this natural talent to help build up our community, churches, and schools?

- Setting a great example—As entrepreneurs we are used to modeling good behavior for our employees. It is equally important to model responsible stewardship and leadership in our community. We never know who is watching us, but we can be sure that *someone* is and they can become motivated and inspired by our example.

- Leverage our professional skills and contacts—Every industry and occupation has unique skills and talents to be used to help others. For example, medical professionals often travel to underdeveloped areas to provide free medical care. For each of us, there is a cause or organization in need of our professional abilities. It is good stewardship to seek them out and serve.

Now a word to all of you self-made men and women out there: Good for you!

It's great that you made your own way, pulled yourself up by your own bootstraps and found a way to succeed all by yourself without help from anyone else. Now what? If you are expecting a medal or a parade, you may find yourself waiting a long time. You see, while your accomplishments may be noteworthy, they are not unique. History is full of stories like yours (and mine)—it's just that hardly anyone remembers. If you want to be remembered, become a great steward of what you have and who you are.

Winston Churchill captured the true spirit of stewardship when he said,

"You make a living by what you get, but you make a life by what you give."

Growing Forward

Think hard about everything you have been given along the way up to now. Look around and decide how you can best become a good steward of all you are and all you have. Then, start making your decisions based on what you can contribute to the lives of other people.

Treasure This

"From everyone who has been given much, much will be required; and to whom they entrusted much, of him they will ask all the more."
Luke 12:48b, NASB

"At times our own light goes out and is rekindled by a spark from another person. Each of us has cause to think with deep gratitude of those who have lighted the flame within us."
Albert Schweitzer

"The hardest arithmetic to master is that which enables us to count our blessings."
Eric Hoffer

41

Kindness

Food for Our Heart

The date was August 18, 1979 and it was a Friday. I was a 24-year-old newlywed of six months. My wife Jane and I had settled into a wonderful routine that included a special date night together on my one day off each week.

I remember I'd gotten up late, thrown on a wrinkled polo shirt and some tennis shorts along with my favorite pair of old, worn-out sneakers. Since I was planning to wax my car before Jane got home from work, I hadn't bothered to clean myself up. Then, realizing I was out of cash, I drove over to the Steak & Ale Restaurant where I worked as a manager to cash a $20 check and get some gas. I walked into the restaurant bar area and found our bartender cleaning up after the lunch rush. I handed him my check and just as he returned with my money, I felt someone tapping me on the shoulder. I turned around to face two men sporting short haircuts, dark suits, and very serious expressions. One was very young (maybe even younger than me). The other appeared to be in his fifties with a real no B.S. look about him.

"Can I help you guys?" I said.

"Are you the manager of this place?" said no B.S. guy.

I extended my hand in greeting, smiled, and replied "Yes I am. My name is Tony Ford, and I'm the General Manager."

Ignoring my proffered greeting, his next words caught me totally by surprise. "We are with the Oklahoma Alcohol Control Board. Turn around and put your hands behind your back. You are under arrest for operating an open saloon in the State of Oklahoma." I just stood there in stunned silence.

In the late 1970s, Oklahoma held the distinction of being one of only two states in the country where "liquor by the drink" was still illegal. To work around this restriction, restaurants and clubs were required to issue their patrons "memberships" which then qualified the establishment as a private club in compliance with state alcohol control statutes. Each year, the state would pick one or two high-profile restaurants to use as examples of non-compliance. All that was required to fail the test was for one person to be served an alcoholic beverage without a proper membership card. Apparently, 1979 was our lucky year because we were selected out of more than 3,000 restaurants to be made that year's example, and I was to be the poster boy!

All of the things that happened next are just a blur. Somehow the man managed to turn me around, secure my wrists in handcuffs, and march me out the front door and into the back of their waiting unmarked government car.

Next came the depressing cavalcade of procedures known in the criminal justice system as processing in. I was searched, and stripped of my wallet, watch, wedding ring, belt, sunglasses and shoestrings. I was photographed, fingerprinted, Mirandized, and thrown into a holding cell containing eight other men of varying ages, sizes, and levels of sobriety.

At about 8:00 that night, I was told that my company had sent our local corporate lawyer down to bail me out. I collected my belongings, called a cab, and went home. For what seemed like an eternity, I stood in the shower trying to wash away the accumulated grime and discouragement of the last few hours. I just wanted to forget the whole ordeal.

The rest of that evening and throughout the next day, Jane and I talked about what had happened and were finally able to set it aside. Still, in the back of my mind, I had two concerns: first, legally—what would happen next? And second, relationally—what would all of our friends think about this? I hoped they would never find out.

I got up early the next morning and particularly appreciated the cool fresh air as I went out front to get the newspaper. After pouring myself a steaming cup of fresh coffee, I opened the paper to see my own face staring back at me. While this Tony looked very scruffy and unkempt, the likeness was still very much me – on the front page of the Tulsa Tribune.

Back then, we were members of Memorial Baptist Church. It was a large Southern Baptist congregation, but we had made most of our friends among the other newlywed couples in our Sunday School class. When we walked into our classroom that next Sunday, I fully expected to get a hard time from the other guys for getting thrown in the pokey. I also thought that many of the other class members would point out that "dancing and drinking" (much less running a saloon) were not in keeping with the doctrines of our church. I just knew that a whole bunch of condemnation was about to hit me. What happened next totally surprised me.

Almost immediately, we were surrounded by our teachers and classmates. We were inundated with questions like "Are you two ok?" and "Is there anything that we can do to help?" and "Would you like to come over to our house for lunch after church?" Eventually, someone pulled out a copy of the newspaper photo and folks began to rib me about doing a better job of representing the class: "Hey Tony, next time you get thrown in jail, at least wear a tie" and "Couldn't you have at least shaved?" and "Tony, you really need a haircut – I hear those prison barbers know their stuff." All in good fun.

Since that time, Jane and I have witnessed many more examples of individual and community kindness poured out on us and on others. As business owners, we have made it a high value in our companies and among our leaders. Here are some of the practical ways that we express kindness within our company culture:

- Patience—Everyone develops and grows in their own time and in their own way. We model kindness when we support that growth and find creative ways to stimulate our employees' natural motivations and abilities.

- Mercy—No one gets it right every time. As leaders, we express kindness when we choose to use mistakes as teaching moments instead of as opportunities to chastise and rebuke people. There is plenty of judgment in the world already—a little mercy goes a long way.

- Wisdom—One thing is true of all of us—we don't know what we don't know. Those of us who have been around awhile show kindness by sharing the wisdom of our past experiences with those who are coming up behind us. Don't be afraid to share your own failures as an example to keep others out of trouble.

- Gentleness—Often as we share important insights, how we say things is just as important as what we say. Leaders model kindness by choosing an appropriate tone and timing for sharing with others.

- Service—From time to time, we are too weak or tired to carry our own loads. Kindness is demonstrated through acts of service in which we carry the load for others until they can take it back themselves.

- Generosity—Employees sometimes find themselves short of resources, in bad relationships, or in need of sound advice. As entrepreneurs, we transact kindness by how we employ the time and resources in our control. Generosity mixed with a little tough love goes a long way in helping others make their lives work.

- Humility—We are all in this together. Life has a way of leveling the playing field when it comes to needs, tragedy, embarrassment, discouragement, and pain. We push kindness to the top of our values list when we live in the attitude of "But for the grace of God, there go I." Kindness flourishes in humility.

Oh, and about my problems with the law. Within a few months, the charges against me were dismissed. It seems that making an example out of someone was the real point of the exercise after all.

The example I will remember is everyone's kindness!

Growing Forward

Reflect on the nature of kindness this week. Ask yourself, "What am I doing as a leader to make kindness a high value in my family and company?" Then, start incorporating some of these ideas where you can. No matter how it changes the folks you serve, kindness is sure to change you!

Treasure This

"Be kind to one another, compassionate, forgiving each other, just as God in Christ also has forgiven you."
Ephesians 4:32, NASB

"Today I bent the truth to be kind, and I have no regret, for I am far surer of what is kind than I am of what is true."
Robert Brault

"If you haven't any charity in your heart, you have the worst kind of heart trouble."
Bob Hope

SECTION SIX

ABUNDANT LIVING

42

Simple Living

Learning to Travel Light

Incredible. Absolutely incredible—but brief!

Those were the words that cycled through my mind as our van topped the ridge line for the first (and last) time, and the Blue Ridge Mountains filled the windshield with the blazing colors of August in North Carolina. Then, just as quickly as it had appeared, the brilliant view vanished into the twilight darkness of triple-canopy tree growth as we plunged back down into the depths of the Pisgah National Forest. For the next nine days, this would be our campus.

Welcome to the North Carolina Outward Bound School.

After another hour of bumping and twisting our way deep into the bowels of the high forest, the blacktop road gave way to what became little more than a cow path. The path meandered up to a small meadow where we finally stopped and unloaded our gear. It was at this juncture I received my first lesson in NCOBS culture—keep it simple and travel light.

Months before the trip began, each of us received a packing list including all of the clothes, gear, and first aid supplies we were required to bring with us. The list was extensive and it took several trips to the sporting goods store to track it all down. Now, each of us was instructed to take all of these items out of our duffle bags and dump them on the ground.

For the next fifteen minutes, our instructors walked around telling us which items to put into one of two separate piles. Quickly, one pile grew as the other diminished. Then the instructors handed out our backpacks and told us to take the small pile and put it into our backpacks, everything else went back into the duffels. Most of us just stood there in a state of stunned silence and confusion.

Finally someone yelled, "Hey—don't you mean to put the small pile in the duffle bag and the big pile in the backpacks?" With a knowing grin on her face, our lead instructor yelled back, "We are only going out for nine days, not six months. You don't need to be hauling around all of that junk. It will just wear you out faster!"

Up until then, I had not paid much attention to what was in my small pile. But now I saw it only contained one pair of spare underwear, one extra t-shirt, one pair of clean socks, and one tube of sunblock. One, one, one of everything and no toilet paper or soap. So, thinking I could get our younger instructor to cut me a little slack in the underwear department, I asked if I could bring another pair. She rolled her eyes and said, "You don't get it, by the time you need more than one extra pair of underwear, we will either be back or you just won't care!" I learned later on that she was right.

Then it started to rain.

For the next nine days, we hiked, climbed, rappelled, ate, drank, and slept in the rain. It rained hard, and it never let up. Only the backs of our eyeballs stayed dry. By the end of the trip even our brains were floating around in a puddle of rainwater.

After a few days, our lives got really simple. It was all about staying as warm and dry as possible (dry meaning not as wet). Nighttime was the worst because when we stopped moving, we stopped creating our own heat.

This brings me to the second thing I learned on Outward Bound— It's ok to be wet and it's ok to be cold, but it's not ok to be wet *and* cold! On several occasions, we had the opportunity to use our new found training to help each other stave off hypothermia.

I learned many other lessons during my soggy sojourn out in the forest: the value of teamwork, the joy of overcoming real fear, and the sense of accomplishment that comes with pushing past your limits. But the greatest lesson that I took away is one that we learned on that first day. Keep it simple—travel light.

As entrepreneurs and leaders, we are responsible for making decisions about how our company outfits itself to perform, compete, and grow. The more processes, rules, procedures, manuals, equipment, real estate, staff, inventory, etc., we accumulate along the way, the more it weighs us down. Here are some practical ways I have found to keep our company's backpack light and manageable:

- Pack light—Keep a close eye on inventory turnover. Most companies have far too much money tied up in dead inventory. If a product is not selling, mark it down and get it off of your shelf. Teach your sales representatives to sell what you have and don't try to stock everything all of the time. Remember, you often make your profit by how and what you buy, not just what you sell. Buy smart.

- Lead the way—Seek out vendors who continually bring in new and exciting products and services. Every time you offer your customers these kinds of products, you separate yourself from the competition and reinforce their desire to give you their business.

- Leave no trace—Teach your people to only buy the supplies and products they need to get their jobs done in the foreseeable future. Excess supplies require extra shelves, closets, and warehouse space. Let your vendors store this stuff on their nickel. Cut the clutter and cut down on the waste. Don't leave a mess lying around.

- Move forward as a team—Everyone has bad days (and sometimes weeks). Make it a part of your company culture to know each other's rhythms and choose together to carry each other's pack when necessary. Make getting to the goal as a group a high value among your people.

- Lead from the front—As the leader, it is your job to set the pace that everyone else will follow. Make it a point to set an aggressive enough pace to ensure high growth while still being attainable and sustainable by your team members.

- Swap packs once in a while—Everyone benefits from gaining a fresh perspective. Take advantage of slow times in your business cycle to cross-train as many employees as possible. When the trail gets steep and muddy, you will be glad you did.

- Go jump in the lake—Life is too short to not have fun as we work. Make time and opportunities to have fun with your people. Give them friendly competitions to focus their energies and harness their playful imagination. Most of all, set an example by not taking yourself too seriously. Unless you run an emergency room, police station, or fire department, keep in mind that this business is not a life and death thing. Have fun!

Growing Forward

Take time this week to consider how you can influence your company in ways that make your corporate journey together more fun, impactful and profitable. Then, fill your own backpack with useful tools to make it happen. Perhaps even include a team-building camping trip or *ropes course.*

But don't forget to check the weather forecast (their attitudes) first.

Treasure This

"Therefore, since we also have such a great cloud of witnesses surrounding us, let's rid ourselves of every obstacle and the sin which so easily entangles us, and let's run with endurance the race that is set before us,"
Hebrews 12:1, NASB

"To serve, to strive, and not to yield."
Outward Bound Motto

"Teamwork is the ability to work together toward a common vision, the ability to direct individual accomplishments toward organizational objectives. It is the fuel that allows common people to attain uncommon results."
Andrew Carnegie

43

Authentic Living

Being Your Real Self

One Sunday morning, my wife Jane and I were driving to church when we came upon a scene that is all too familiar out here in the country: buzzards circling over a dead skunk. The reason we knew it was a dead skunk was the way the smell instantly invaded our car, even though the windows were up and the air conditioning was on.

I turned and said to Jane, "It is amazing to me that even buzzards can eat a dead skunk. They must not have any sense of smell at all!"

Jane remarked, "Well, their sense of smell may not be very good, but I'll bet there is nothing wrong with their taste buds."

I replied, "How can you say that? The taste must be worse than the smell."

With a grin, she responded, "Well, I guess it's just a matter of what you grew up eating!"

Yuck! But she was right.

While this is a somewhat foul example, the point is nevertheless true; we are indeed the product of our upbringing. Skunks are skunks, and buzzards are buzzards, and they live out what they are in nature's circle of life without confusion or complaint. They simply are what they are.

If only it could be that simple for us humans.

How we are raised has a tremendous influence on how we view ourselves and how others view us. Unlike animals who seem to be hardwired to accept their role in life, we tend to allow outside influences to dictate our behavior. It is at this point that a lot of our confusion and heartache begins. It is here we make a choice to live out either our natural or adapted behaviors.

Allow me to explain the difference.

Our natural behavior is the person we were born to be. In other words, our personality traits, natural skills, and gifts, likes and dislikes all move us toward acting and reacting to the world in a certain way. It is the person we are without having to think about it. If we got up each morning and just went to work and did what came naturally to us—this would be our natural behavior.

Our adapted behavior is the person we have learned to be. These are the behaviors, actions, activities, motivations and ways of interacting that have been taught to us by the people who raised us, and played with us as we grew up. This is the role we and others have cast us in over time.

In my own life, I have always been cast in the role of leader. Since childhood, I have been physically bigger than my peers, naturally task-oriented and aggressive. The people around me have witnessed these traits and posited that I should take a leadership role because of them. Consequently, I have operated as a leader and entrepreneur for most of my life. This then has become my adapted behavior.

While in point of fact leadership does come very naturally to me, it is not really my natural behavior. A very large part of my personality is playful, creative, fun-loving, and irreverent. Occupationally, my *natural behavior* might push me toward being a teacher or entertainer much more than a leader. So what happened?

As we move through life, there is a constant tension between our adapted and natural behaviors. If we can find relationships, occupations, hobbies, and roles that allow our natural behavior to find expression, the tension is manageable. However, when our natural behavior becomes more and more suppressed due to the demands of our adapted behavior, we quickly become very unhappy and frustrated. It is for this reason that the longer we live in our "adapted life", the less we enjoy it.

Living in conflict between who we have to be and who we were meant to be is at the heart of many problems we face. Depression, anxiety, fatigue, even divorce (and a host of other interpersonal struggles) are caused or made worse by this situation. The longer it goes unresolved, the more negatively it impacts the quality of our lives.

Just like for others, as leaders and entrepreneurs, this type of internal conflict becomes very destructive to our family, business and personal relationships. But for us, the demands of needing to have all the answers and wearing numerous hats sometimes makes it almost impossible to manage.

Here are a few things to consider if you are wrestling with this situation right now:

- Remember that you have choices—As Frank Sinatra was fond of singing, "I did it my way." Being the boss or owner is not worth much if you can't operate out of your own skin. Try giving yourself permission to relax a little more and allow yourself some "me time" away from the business. Use this time to get in touch with what you really want out of life. Then start making choices to reinforce those desires.

- Focus on your natural strengths—If you think about it, you know what activities and abilities come naturally to you. Make a list of what you instinctively do well. Then, make another list of all the things that are a real discipline and that you may not be all that good at. This is the list that describes the people you need around you to maximize who you really are. Now, go find them. (Or they may already be in your organization—don't forget to look there first).

- Start pushing back—Now that you are all grown up, don't forget that the you everyone knows is the product of many years of adapting to other people's expectations. Never expect others to see the natural you without some help. The best way to make the transition is to start gently pushing back when others dump expectations or demands on you that move you farther away from the person you naturally are. Be careful not to push back too hard. Remember, you did not adopt these behaviors overnight, and it will take time to move in a more natural direction.

- Find a coach/mentor—Now is a critical time to enter into an accountability relationship with an older, more experienced person. It takes someone who cares enough about you to tell you the truth to also keep this transition process on track and moving forward. Once you find the right person, do your best to become totally transparent with them. The better your coach/mentor knows who you naturally are, the better he or she will be able to guide you on your journey of discovery.

- Don't stop until you are finished—As hard as it is to commit to finding out who you naturally are, it is even harder to make a full and complete transition. The changes will be hard on you, your family, your company, and maybe even your bank account. In my experience, many entrepreneurs work out of their adapted behavior because it pays better than their natural gifting. The problem with this is while they are able to gather up a lot more money and stuff; their high stress level of not living out who they naturally are keeps them from enjoying it. What a cruel contradiction. My advice (and I have done this myself) is to reclaim who you really are and not stop until the transformation is accomplished.

For me, authentic living is simply getting and staying in touch with who God meant for me to be. When I find myself weighed down with activities and behaviors based on the expectations of others and not my own natural skills and gifts, I stop and reassess what I am doing. I work hard to serve others through my natural gifts, but I am no longer confused about who I am and what I am supposed to be doing with my life.

Choose to get back in touch with and pursue the natural you!

Growing Forward

Take some time away from work this week to consider these concepts. Make a list of your natural gifts and also those things that are a real struggle. Find a coach/mentor and work together to create a plan for next steps. It will be a natural fit!

Treasure This

"Do you see a person skilled in his work? He will stand before kings; He will not stand before obscure people."
Proverbs 22:29, NASB

"Be yourself. No one can ever tell you you're doing it wrong."
Author Unknown

"Love yourself first and everything else falls into line. You really have to love yourself to get anything done in this world."
Author Unknown

44

Physical Health

You Have One Body, Make Your Choices

One of my lifelong friends is the pastor of a local church. When his sermon topic deals with money, raising children, or how much we eat, he warns his flock to "Put on your tough shirts because I just stopped preaching and started meddling."

While it is not my intention to make anyone feel uncomfortably self-conscious about how we eat or how much/how little we exercise, as entrepreneurs our bodies are the basic tool of our trade. People look upon our general state of well-being and make assumptions about our habits, beliefs, abilities, and decision-making skills. For better or worse, our level of physical fitness dictates (to some extent) how we experience the world and how people interact with us.

To make the situation even more complicated, there are also the issues of how much rest we get, and the things we put into our bodies besides good foods (substance abuse). All of these practices have a major impact on how our minds and bodies function on a daily basis. Remember, as leaders we are paid to make great decisions based on the information available. Anything that artificially short-circuits our brains works against us.

In my experience, everyone has a "drug of choice." My drug of choice is food. If I do not focus my attention on what and how much I eat, in no time my weight goes up like a rocket. I know other entrepreneurs whose drug of choice is alcohol, porn, gambling, crack, pot, methamphetamine, prescription drugs, work, etc. Each person (and their families) is living with the fall-out of their addictions. Their companies suffer dramatic negative effects as well since the leader is distracted from his duties by these outside influences.

Additionally, we do not have to have a serious substance abuse problem to forfeit our effectiveness. Chronic pain, lack of sleep and issues like hypertension are all just as self-defeating.

Since so much of what comes our way physically is out of our control, it only makes sense for us to purposely do good things for our bodies. These things include:

- Getting proper rest every night.
- Coming to grips with what our body is telling us when we feel run down or overwhelmed.
- Taking time off from work to balance our business and family lives.
- Deciding how much is enough when it comes to growing our business and financial obligations.

The human body is a truly miraculous creation. However, it has built-in limitations. We can push these limits for short periods of time with relatively little damage. But when we adopt excessive practices as our normal lifestyle, something has to give.

So, ask yourself, how well am I taking care of my body?

Since self-awareness is not always a common attribute of busy entrepreneurs, we may not already be cognizant of what issues need more attention. Now, just as you plan your business activities, you can elevate "self-preservation" to a higher position on your planning priority list. Some of these to-dos may include:

- Work out for 30 minutes three times per week (at home or at the gym).
- Get some advice on foods that give you more energy, even out your blood sugar and lower your cholesterol.
- Join a peer group to lose that last 15 lbs. of "baby fat."
- Make an annual appointment with your doctor to have a full physical.
- Schedule a vacation—a real vacation with no laptops allowed!
- Allow yourself to take two full days off at least every other week.
- Get help for any chronic pain or addiction issues.
- Talk to a counselor about any feelings of depression (you are not alone!).

Even though my pastor friend is charged with helping folks grow spiritually, he often reminds me:

"If you mess up your body—where are you going to live?"

Growing Forward

If you are like me, the last thing you need is another to-do on your list. But, this is serious stuff. After all, pretty much all of your plans hinge on having reasonably good health. So pick just one of the eight suggestions listed above and commit to starting on it this week. After you have built some good habits around that one, pick another. Before long you will see some real positive changes in the way you feel, look, and enjoy life.

Treasure This

"Or do you not know that your body is the temple of the Holy Spirit within you, who you have from God, and that you are not your own? For you have been bought for a price: therefore glorify God in your body."
1 Corinthians 6:19-20, NASB

"In health there is freedom. Health is the first of all liberties."
Henri Frederic Amiel

"Health is not valued until sickness comes."
Thomas Fuller

45

Marriage

///

Practice, Practice, Practice

For many years, my wife Jane and I have had the privilege of mentoring and discipling dozens of newlywed couples in our home. On average, we meet with them every week for two hours at a time. Each group of four to seven couples participates for about two years. During one of those years, I was a young hospital chaplain at Baylor University Medical Center in Dallas.

A little while after being assigned to the Cardiac Intensive Care Unit, I asked a doctor friend why doctors refer to their work as a "practice." He grinned and said, "Because if we ever get all of these diseases figured out, no one will be sick anymore, and we will go from practice to out-of-business overnight! I had to noodle on that one for a while.

I finally figured out that he was saying no matter how good a doctor becomes; medicine, the human body, and diseases are all constantly changing and requiring new and better solutions. After more than four decades of practice, I have come to the same conclusions about marriage. It is just too complicated and evolves too fast for anyone to really master it. The best we can hope for is to keep learning and growing in it as we move along together.

Now I know what some of you newlyweds may be thinking. "If this guy does not know what's up with marriage after 44 years, how are we going to make it work? Well, relax, because it is not as hard as it sounds. However, marriage does require a bit of practice (make that lots of practice) to get the hang of it.

We could fill an entire library with all of the books written about marriage over the years. But to save you some time, here are just a few of the habits Jane and I have found really helpful for building a long and happy marriage:

- Commitment—Decide before you say "I do" that marriage is for life. Not unlike building muscles through exercise, marriage only gets stronger if you work at it consistently. Every second spent asking, "What if?" is just another second wasted on working out solutions and moving your marriage forward. If divorce is an option for either one of you going into your marriage, take my advice – change your mindset or start dating again, because you are not ready to have a long term committed marriage.

- Couples—Marriage is about becoming a highly functional team. While you may feel like you are giving up your independence, the goal is learning how to become effectively interdependent with your spouse. When done right, one plus one equals more than two. The best place to learn how to become a more effective team is to hang out with other great couples. Church marriage groups, discipleship classes and marriage enrichment conferences are great places to look!

- Courage—It takes courage to get your needs met in a marriage. It takes no courage to be an abuser or to become a doormat. Expect and provide respect and security to your spouse. If cut-downs are your way of relating to each other, at least have the courage to admit that you need to find a more supportive and encouraging way to communicate. Go get some counseling and start as soon as you can.

- Conversation—Married couples can gauge their intimacy by how many things are on the "We don't talk about that" list. Chances are these subjects were difficult for one or both of you to discuss before you got married. It only gets harder the longer you wait. Again, find someone you both trust and work on bringing these issues out into the open.

- Common Goals—Couples either grow together toward a mutual goal, or they grow apart as they pursue other things (things that could lead to emotional or physical affairs). Our marriage has always been centered on growing to become more like Jesus Christ as individuals. As we grow closer to Him, we grow closer to each other.

- Children—It is always best for children to have grown-ups for parents. Just because you may be chronologically adult, does not mean you are mature in all areas of your life. When considering having children, it is critical to work even harder on your marriage. The prettiest baby room in the world does not compare to the value of a solid marriage in raising a child. My advice? Skip the fancy wallpaper and enroll in a child-rearing class at your church or public health department.

Remember, you need to engage with other couples to encourage and strengthen your marriage!

Growing Forward

Great marriages do not happen by accident. They evolve and mature as a result of hard work and purposeful planning. They also do not grow in a vacuum. All couples endure hardships, losses, and defeats. While some couples fall apart under these conditions, committed couples draw closer to each other, to their friends, to their families, and to God.

Treasure This

"For this reason a man will leave his father and mother and be united to his wife, and the two shall become one flesh."
Ephesians 5:31, NASB

"A successful marriage requires falling in love many times, always with the same person."
Mignon McLaughlin

"It is not a lack of love, but a lack of friendship that makes unhappy marriages."
Friedrich Nietzsche

46

Faith

The Treasure We Find at the End of Ourselves

Many folks think an author sits down to write a book and then moves from the first chapter to the second and so on until it is finished (and maybe some do). However, my practice has been to wake up each morning, drink my coffee out on the back porch with Samson and Goliath (my faithful hounds), and wait for inspiration and consciousness to arrive. On some days, it simply never happens. On others, I cannot get the words down on paper fast enough to keep up.

Until all of the chapters are finished, edited, critiqued, and handed back to me to be re-written, the whole thing is simply an exercise in faith! Of course, the fact that you are now reading this book means I finally finished.

It is no accident that I am just now getting around to writing about faith. You see, I have been avoiding it for years using a variety of reasons and excuses. Some of my favorites have been:

- Faith is an article of religion—I may offend non-religious people.

- Faith is not something one can prove—I may sound ignorant or uninformed.
- Faith is active—Even when I see it at work, I feel inadequate to describe its power.
- Faith is very personal—I can't presume to know how my readers feel about it.
- Faith is necessary—I can't comprehend living without it.

Obviously, all of these excuses are about my own inadequacies and not about the topic itself. But when it comes right down to it, faith is a BIG subject! With this in mind, I can only hope to offer up what my experience with faith has been and leave it to you to draw your own personal conclusions and applications. Fair enough? Good.

In describing my experience of faith, I titled this chapter "The treasure we find at the end of ourselves." For me, faith is the purest expression of love that we as humans can extend to God and to others. It is our way of saying, "I trust you unconditionally, and if you don't come through, I have no safety net." This kind of trust can only exist in a relationship marked by unconditional love. The Bible defines faith like this:

"What is faith? It is the confident assurance that what we hope for is going to happen. It is the evidence of things we cannot see" (Hebrews 11:1, NLT).

As an entrepreneur, leader, husband, and father, I understand many people expect me to make sure certain things happen for them. They have faith in *me*. These are my responsibilities as I live out my relationships and roles in the community. But it begs the question: "With everyone counting on me—who do I get to count on?" The Bible says by faith, I can count on God for things I hope for in the future but cannot see in the present. This includes the ability to fulfill my obligations to others.

For the most part, when people talk about faith, it is in the context of our relationship and dependence on God. But there are many other aspects of faith that have more to do with how we relate to each other as husbands, wives, children, bosses, employees, etc.

As a husband, I exercise my faith by how I serve my wife. It is my role to honor her by putting her ahead of myself and others. I am also charged with caring for her physical, emotional, and spiritual needs. It is my joy and obligation to ensure she always understands and feels loved by me in the same way Christ loved the church and sacrificed his life for her.

As a father, I model my faith by how I live my life as an example to our two sons, Michael and Daniel. When I make mistakes that affect them, it is my job to confess it to them and ask for forgiveness. When I have successes, it is my role to demonstrate how to share the glory of them with others. On those occasions when the boys need to be corrected or disciplined in order to understand right from wrong, I have faith that long after they have stopped being mad at me for disciplining them, they will remember the lesson and use it to stay out of future trouble.

As an entrepreneur, if I take my faith seriously, it will change how I treat other people. I will establish a company culture where people are encouraged to trust the leadership and each other (even if it takes years to build). I will find creative ways to serve not only my customers but also my employees and vendors as well. I will live out my faith in the community by using the resources of the business to give back. I will operate the business as a servant leader and model good stewardship practices to teach my people how to take care of what has been entrusted to us.

From personal experience, I can also tell you here are some very practical and profound benefits to be derived from having faith in God and in others, including:

- Contentment—Having faith that God will always provide for my needs (not necessarily my wants) takes a tremendous amount of weight off my shoulders.

- Transparency—Faith tells me God knows me just as I am with all of my faults, and he still wants the best for me. That truth allows me to be open and transparent with others who can also accept me just as I am.

- Peace—Faith provides "The peace that passes all understanding." This is a spiritual understanding that assures me in my darkest times everything will turn out okay in the end.

- Joy—Faith allows me to look to the future with positive anticipation, believing that tomorrow will be better than today and filled with opportunities.

In my life, I have experienced many great gains and losses. I have endured years of chronic pain and enjoyed the love and faithfulness of a wonderful family. Through it all, there was faith.

Till the end and even past it – I believe that faith will always prevail over doubt!

Growing Forward

In the best of times, living out our responsibilities as leaders, entrepreneurs, parents, and spouses can be very difficult. It takes a lot of faith to face life with a positive attitude. Take some time this week to consider where you have chosen to place your faith. If you are like most folks, you have spread your faith around between your own abilities, other people you trust, and to a greater or lesser extent, God. I encourage you to think about how the present arrangement is working out and to consciously decide if your faith is totally invested in the right place.

Treasure This

"Now faith is the substance of things hoped for, the evidence of things not seen."
Hebrews 11:1, KJV

"We are never defeated unless we give up on God."
Ronald Reagan

"Belief is a wise wager. Granted that faith cannot be proved, what harm will come to you if you gamble on its truth and it proves false? If you gain, you gain all; if you lose, you lose nothing. Wager, then, without hesitation, that He exists."
Blaise Pascal

47

Fear

Honoring the Threat and Moving Past It

Fear.

Just the word brings up feelings of dread, darkness, and anxiety. It is tangled up with words like failure, danger, inadequacy, and abuse. It is the last stop when our best ideas fall short, and our last measure of hope has vanished.

The Bible says that fear is the opposite of faith. In this context, faith in God prevents us from depending on ourselves for all of life's solutions, trusting God loves us as a good parent loves their children and will protect them at all costs.

Our own life experiences teach us that most of what we feel as fear is the anticipation of bad things which may or may not happen to us in the future. Looking back, we see the actual dreaded event we're imagining is not nearly as painful as the awful scenarios our minds conjure up.

For the entrepreneur, fear is a two-edged sword. On the one edge, fear of the unknown motivates us to do our due diligence before moving forward in a business deal. Fear of loss drives us forward when our hope of gain has been completely exhausted. In this sense, if properly understood, fear can be a useful tool.

On the other edge of the blade, fear is an emotion that is hard to hide and very easy to pass on to others—particularly our employees. When the boss comes through the door in the morning with "that worried look," everyone in the building knows about it before their first cup of coffee. Just as enthusiasm is contagious and encouraging, fear can become debilitating to an otherwise healthy organization.

So what exactly do we do with our fears? The short answer is everything—and also nothing.

The 'everything' includes giving ourselves permission to be people first and leaders second. We are whole personalities, and must recognize everything that happens to us personally will affect us professionally in some way. For this reason, it is critical to maintain a healthy balance between our professional and personal lives. Work hard, yes. Play hard, yes. But play with family and friends who actively affirm us and refill our emotional fuel tanks on a regular basis. Healthy relationships are our best defense against allowing excessive fear into our lives.

The 'nothing' is about learning to become more patient. Since our own life experience teaches us that many if not most fears never actually materialize, with age and practice, we can learn to "not sweat the small stuff" so much. We can also take courage that we have already built a history of overcoming difficult situations and bringing ourselves and our people through to victory.

Whether we are trusting in God, other people or our own life experiences and abilities, as long as we do business in a complex world, fear will be a part of the equation.

Leaders are required to identify and honor threats that come at their organization and family. The ability to embrace these fears with courage, determination, and rational decision-making allows us to move past them. These skills should be a part of every leader's tool chest.

We must learn to master our fears —or they will surely master us!

Growing Forward

Take time this week to make a list of things you fear. Be specific about people, dates, and situations. Then, set an appointment with yourself in one month to review the list. I think you may be surprised at how many situations have resolved themselves with little or no intervention from you.

Treasure This

"Even though I walk through the valley of the shadow of death, I will fear no evil, for you are with me; your rod and your staff, they comfort me."
Psalm 23:4, NASB

"I have learned over the years that when one's mind is made up, this diminishes fear; knowing what must be done does away with fear."
Rosa Parks

"You gain strength, courage, and confidence by every experience in which you really stop to look fear in the face. You must do the thing which you think you cannot do."
Eleanor Roosevelt

48

Retirement

The Gateway to Finishing Well

I have heard it said, *If you find something you love to do, you will never have to work a day in your life.* I take this to mean that our goal should be to find work so well matched to our personality and skills that it is really fun to do. While I don't disagree with the sentiment, I do wonder if it is a practical undertaking. After all, if work does not *stretch* us by making us try things we are uncomfortable with, how are we to grow?

How we view work has a lot to do with how we understand the concept of retirement. Just as we desire to do work that is almost a perfect fit, we may also want to plan for and participate in the "perfect retirement." If this is true for you, have you ever really stopped to think about the goal of retirement?

For many, retirement is all about having no responsibilities, financial freedom, carefree days filled with our favorite hobbies, travel, relaxation and no more work. Many folks think of retirement as their chance to get off of the merry-go-round and just drop out.

Twenty-eight years ago, I had the opportunity to just drop out. I was 40 years old and had reached a place where our company could afford to continue to pay me even though I made relatively small contributions to its daily operations. But there were two major problems:

1. I had just been run over by a boat and had to spend my days and nights in chronic pain.

2. Along with losing my ability to think critically and function effectively as a leader, I also lost my ability to really enjoy life.

The good news is that after nine years, medical technology caught up to my condition, and I was able to have surgery to replace my broken parts with new, artificial ones and return to work. Like the song says: "You don't know what you've got, 'til it's gone!"

Now, I am not trying to equate a well-planned retirement strategy with being forced into a sedentary lifestyle by an injurious accident. What I am pointing out is just because we make plans for retiring in a certain manner does not always mean the future will work out that way. With that in mind, consider asking yourself a few critical questions about your retirement:

- **Do I even want to retire?** If you enjoy the work you do and you are making a meaningful contribution to the world around you, why stop? After my accident, I lived with what felt like no purposeful work for several years. Doing meaningful work is much more fun and holds more interest for me than just sitting around. My new concept of retirement is all about giving back instead of giving up.

- **What is my plan if I have to stop working before I want to?** More people are forced to stop working because of health-related problems than you would think. Look around and determine how you would invest your time if you could not work in your present occupation. I chose to do more mentoring, teaching, and writing, and it has become a way of life. Plan for the worst, and pray for the best.

- **If I do retire, what will that look like?** This is where you have to be both very honest and specific. Let's face it, we can only stand so much of a good thing (hunting, fishing, golf, etc.). Everyone needs purpose in their daily lives to feel fulfilled. Identify what your days and weeks would be used for to ensure that the winter season of your life is the best it can possibly be.

- **Find help to become helpful.** Most of us focus only on the financial aspects of retirement. Local charities, universities, volunteer organizations, hospitals, and churches all have a wealth of information about how we can make a meaningful contribution by mentoring, teaching, facilitating, and generally giving back to our community.

Remember, retirement is not required to ensure a significant life—finishing well is!

Growing Forward

I find it sad that so many people live their lives waiting to retire. Instead of developing the interests, relationships, and skills needed to enjoy their lives in the present, they accept the notion that retirement is some magical place where all of the stresses and aggravations of life somehow disappear. From my worldview, that place is not called retirement; it's called Heaven.

While we are still alive and kicking, it is probably a good thing to actively plan and prepare ourselves for both.

Treasure This

"Whatever you do, work at it with all your heart, as working for the Lord, not for human masters,"
Colossians 3:23, NIV

"Retirement is the ugliest word in the language."
Ernest Hemingway

"Retirement kills more people than hard work ever did."
Malcolm Forbes

SECTION SEVEN

COMMUNITY

49

Encouragement

////

The Gift That Means So Much

It's 1:30 on a cloudy summer afternoon in Texas. I am in my office waiting for the first of my afternoon appointments to arrive. Her name is Wendy. Wendy is an entrepreneur. She is also a breast cancer survivor. For the past seven years, she has had to balance running her business, radiation treatments, chemotherapy, surgeries, raising children, and basic survival. This morning, she found out that the cancer is back.

Now, it is 1:43, and she is still not here. I hope she is ok.

I glance out the window into the parking lot and see Sandy asleep in the passenger's seat of the family van. Sandy and Todd are also customers of ours. Sandy has brain cancer. Her cancer is much more aggressive and advanced than Wendy's. I get a bottle of cold water from our fridge and go out to the car. For the next ten minutes, we visit, and I reassure her she is often in our thoughts and always in our prayers. When I go back into the office, she falls back to sleep, having just come from radiation therapy.

Both Wendy and Sandy share many things in common. Both were moving happily through their lives, doing their jobs and leading others when WHAM—everything fell apart.

Now, they have moved from being wonderful business owners and encouragers to desperately needing encouragement. As Wendy says, "Some days it is only the encouragement of my friends and family that keeps me going; without it, I think I would just die."

Like Wendy and Sandy, I have spent many years on both sides of this process.

As a hospital chaplain working in cardiac intensive care units, I invested my days in encouraging patients, family, and staff members. Later, while starting and growing companies, I became a leader who kept a good face on during difficult situations. But it was not until I moved out of the position of encourager to become the one desperately needing encouragement that I really understood how powerful this activity really is.

In the summer of 1995, I was run over by a personal watercraft while driving my own PWC on a local lake. The other boat rammed into my hip at about 25 miles per hour and launched me into the water several dozen yards away. This accident started a dark 10-year journey through surgeries, chronic pain clinics, massive weekly pain injections, physical therapy, and pain medications.

Until medical technology caught up to the damage in my back and I received two new artificial spinal discs in 2006, my life was a downward spiral of pain, fatigue, and hopelessness. It was the prayers and encouragement of my family (particularly my incredible wife, Jane), friends, employees, and fellow church members who sustained me during this long journey of despair.

It is against the backdrop of this difficult chapter of my life that I now understand the power of encouragement.

As leaders, we are faced with a variety of constantly changing priorities. Personnel problems, vendor issues, customer complaints, and dozens of other factors combine to rob us of our time and drown out our joy. For a long time, I had allowed the day-to-day grind of growing my companies to overshadow the importance of providing consistent encouragement to others. It was not until my own near-fatal accident that I realized the truth in Winston Churchill's words:

"You make a living by what you get. But you make a life by what you give."

With this sentiment in mind, please allow me to suggest several practical ways you can use the gift of encouragement to enrich the lives of others while fortifying your own:

- Never minimize the power of your personal attention to the needs of an employee.
- Build a habit of sending a handwritten thank you card or gift to every person who grants you a meeting with them.
- Take time to sit with your employees, close vendors, and customers when they have a loved one in the hospital having surgery or major illness.
- Build time into your weekly schedule to call and check up on people you know who are going through struggles.
- Volunteer to give free advice or services to leaders who are just getting started.
- Build a culture of real caring into your business by setting an example as you go through your work day.
- Exercise kindness as often as you can.

Encouragement can make a real difference as you give it and receive it—and it's free!

Growing Forward

I have found that there are many more opportunities to encourage others than I had ever imagined in my early career. At the heart of encouragement is "courage," and remembering that courage is an act of the will, I challenge you to take some of these first steps towards becoming an encouragement to others. If you do, I promise that it will change your entrepreneurial journey for the better!

Treasure This

Are you:

Empty? Jesus said "I am the bread of life." - John 6:35, NIV

Stumbling? Jesus said, "I am the light of the world."
John 8:12, NIV

Stressed? Jesus said, "I will give you rest." - Matthew 11:28, NIV

Useless? Jesus said, "I am the true vine." - John 15:1, NIV

Seeking guidance? Jesus said, "I am the good shepherd."
John 10:11, NIV

Alone? Jesus said, "I am with you always." - Matthew 28:20, NIV

Without hope? Jesus said, "I am the resurrection and the life." - John 11:25, NIV

"A word of encouragement from a teacher to a child can change a life. A word of encouragement from a spouse can save a marriage. A word of encouragement from a leader can inspire a person to reach her potential."
John C. Maxwell

"Instead of being critical of people in authority over you and envious of their position, be happy you're not responsible for everything they have to do. Instead of piling on complaints, thank them for what they do. Overwhelm them with encouragement and appreciation!"
Joyce Meyer

50

Effective Networking

How to Become the Go-To Person

Christmas morning, 1963, came early to my house.

We had just moved back to Fort Hood, Texas, after spending three years stationed at Schofield Barracks in Hawaii. My dad was settling into his new job as the Division Artillery Sergeant Major on post and my mom was doing her best to make our new "dependants' quarters" a cozy home for her family. After three years of celebrating Christmas amongst palm trees, we were thrilled to discover a light glaze of frosty snow had covered the brown and gray patch of turf that passed for our front lawn.

As my sister and I attacked our presents, mom and dad sipped on their fresh cups of coffee, and watched carefully for our reactions to the gifts. I remember the remote control tank that exploded into view as I ripped off the wrapping on my "big box present." It was awesome. All olive drab with a huge front cannon, wide, sticky tracks and a 360 degree spinning turret. It even made tank sounds as it moved over everything in its path—old shoes, potted plants, the cat (sorry, Twinkles, that patch of hair will grow back soon, you'll see).

For the next hour and a half, I was in Little Boy Heaven! My tank required eight D batteries to drive its treads and move its turret around while another four C batteries were needed in the remote control. In fact, while my tank could not really destroy anything I shot at, it could have passed as the original *Terminator* when it came to burning through batteries. When the batteries ran out, my wonderful tank became as useless as a tree stump.

For most kids, burning through 12 batteries in 90 minutes would mean "adios playtime" with the new toy—but not for me. You see, at our house, we had an unlimited supply of batteries. Not only that, but they were even all the same color (Army olive drab) and came to us by the box load. So, when my batteries gave up, I simply went to the closet, opened a fresh box, and got busy again.

Because we were plugged into the NCO supply chain, the same unlimited supply status applied to ballpoint pens, toilet paper, small hand tools, and "sea rations" (who's idea was it to put canned fruit cake in these things anyway?).

For you civilians out there, an NCO is a Non-Commissioned Officer (ranked First Sergeant or above). In the military services, these men and women are a very cohesive, tight-knit group who basically see to it that orders are carried out and work gets accomplished.

It is not an exaggeration to say that the NCO corps is the group that gets most things done in the Army, Navy, Marines, Air Force, and Coast Guard. These folks are the military's Go-To People and networkers extraordinaire.

For as long as there has been a military, it has been understood that certain perks come with the territory. Base housing, clothing allowance, moving allowance, combat pay, etc., are official types of sanctioned compensation. Small things like batteries and cheap pens are just some of the "little extras" that seem to show up in abundance when supplies get ordered. Many of these items are sent to the wrong place or are about to expire, so if you are an enterprising Quartermaster, you give them to folks who can use them instead of throwing them away. In return, these people help you keep things moving forward to support the troops when you need them. It's all about getting the job done – in spite of some built in inefficiencies that are part and parcel of huge organizations (and none is bigger than the military).

As entrepreneurs, we also use small "freebies" to enhance our standing and keep our company's name in front of our customers and vendors. These promotional items come in the form of pens, insulated can holders, frisbees, ball caps, and thousands of other specialty items. In fact, handing out this stuff is so easy we often forget the really valuable premium we should be offering is our time and insights.

Just like in the military, it is a big mistake to place too high a value on free batteries and sea rations when we know the flow of information is what really makes things happen. Taking the time to personally interact with our customers, vendors, employees, competitors, and the community can pay big dividends. Here are some very practical ways to become the Go-To Person:

Networking in your own company:

- Learn to sit down at your employee's desks or in the company lunchroom and just talk with them. Find out how things are with their families. Ask about the value of the training and tools they are getting. The key here is being sincere. They will know if you are faking it, so wait until you are in a mood to really listen and then really listen.

- Observe how your employees look, sound, and act. Dramatic changes in their attitudes, manner of dress, punctuality, or weight fluctuation can be clues to important life changes you should be aware of. Personnel problems only get worse when they go unnoticed or unaddressed.

- Walk around the building at least once a month and use the office machines yourself. See if the copier really works or still messes up every other page. Find out if the new headphones sound fuzzy or if the old chair mats need replacing. Just because things are good in your office doesn't mean they are good everywhere else.

- Find ways to do favors for your managers and employees. They will often tell you about things they need if you just ask them. When you do, don't make a big deal of it. It is much better for them to owe YOU a favor than to gain any extra approval from their co-workers. Just go about doing good quietly—the word will get out on its own.

Networking in your industry:

- Schedule a weekly two-minute update call to at least 10 of your customers/vendors. Share one or two valuable pieces of information you have learned to help them in their business. It can be a magazine article you've read or a tidbit from a meeting you attended. The point is to stay in touch with helpful information.

- Go to trade shows with a plan. Stop by every competitor's booth to say hello. Be prepared to share at least two pieces of industry information that will help them without hurting you. The point is to come prepared so that you don't sound uninformed on one hand or sound like a hopeless gossip on the other. Remember, this is business.

- Find a professional group you really enjoy spending time with. Don't settle for just attending meetings; find a fulfilling role and then volunteer for it. This is the perfect platform to allow you to call competitors and industry insiders who would not normally expect to interact with you. Now you are in a position to be in the know when things affecting your company change.

- Position your company for industry recognition. Most trade groups have annual awards for outstanding member performance. Nothing tells your customers you are a great company like a "Distributor of the Year Award" or "Customer Service Award" from your peer companies. This type of recognition can be leveraged into thousands of dollars worth of free publicity.

- Get to know the folks who know what is going on in your industry. Most of the time, these will be the "Old Heads" who have been around since dirt. Your approach to them should be tempered with high amounts of respect and deference. Each will have their own personality quirks (just like we do), but don't let that put you off. Work at trying to understand where they are coming from, and eventually, each will share the insights that put them at the top of the heap in your industry.

- Remember to say thank you. Every time anyone in your industry does something nice for you, be sure to send them a written thank you note. In an era of emails, voicemails, and text messages, nothing expresses authentic appreciation like a hand-written note. Make it kind, thoughtful, and personal. Over time, folks in your industry will start to tell each other about how enjoyable you are to deal with.

Networking in your community:

- Reach out into the community to other business, church, and city leaders who need help with their projects. People like doing business with folks who understand their company is a part of the community and have an obligation to give back. Again, less is more in this regard. Don't exalt your own activities—leave that to others. You will be surprised at how many folks are watching.

- Teach your children the value of doing favors for others. Entrepreneurs come from all walks of life, but a larger percentage come from entrepreneurial families. Second and third-generation business owners who are raised with giving back as a high value tend to add great value to the community.

- Plug your company and your people into community projects. But do these things for the right reasons—to help your friends and neighbors—not just to popularize your company.

- Trust that people are smart enough to know who the good people are when it comes to companies that really care. Over time, your market share and profits will reflect how they appreciate your efforts.

In our businesses, just like in the military, it is up to us to be the Go-To People if we want our company, industry, and community to improve. It is important to always remember our employees, customers, vendors, and neighbors are in this great adventure with us. Together, by looking out for each other, we can build an environment that serves everyone and teaches the right things to the generations following us.

Like my Dad always reminded me, "Treat people right on your first enlistment son, you are going to see them over and over again!".

Growing Forward

Take some time this week to consider how you can incorporate some of these networking concepts into your daily life. Then, keep a close watch on how the people around you react to your new proactive approach. Soon, you will gain a reputation as the Go-To Person in your company and community.

Treasure This

"Let's not become discouraged in doing good, for in due time we will reap, if we do not become weary."
Galatians 6:9, NASB

"Rolodex power. Your power is almost directly proportional to the thickness of your Rolodex and the time you spend maintaining it. Put bluntly, the most potent people I've known have been the best networkers—they 'know everybody from everywhere' and have just been out to lunch with most of them."
Tom Peters

"The successful networkers I know—the ones receiving tons of referrals and feeling truly happy about themselves—continually put the other person's needs ahead of their own."
Bob Burg

51

Loneliness

////

Every Leader's Companion

The songwriters got it right—"One is the loneliest number" and "Only the lonely" know the heartache we feel when we fail at our efforts to lead others.

For anyone who has donned the mantle of leader or entrepreneur and chosen to paddle their own canoe down the raging river of competitive capitalism, the notion of loneliness is ever present. It stalks us after every tough decision and mocks us with every obstacle we fail to overcome. It also reaches out to impact our health, self-respect, and will to go on. It sometimes even invades our personal relationships with disastrous results.

So what can we do to overcome loneliness? I'm glad you asked.

Throughout my career as an entrepreneur and mentor, I've come across many who are lonely. It's a common thread that has entangled all of us at some point. Apparently, it is so common to our leadership experience as to almost hide in the background of the issues, choices and actions we deal with every day. It shows up when we second guess our decisions, lose our tempers, fail to follow up on important opportunities or simply get burned out. Sometimes it takes another person to point out we are stuck in "trying to go it alone" before we recognize just how lonely and isolated we have become.

Loneliness is one of the main reasons I became an Executive Coach at age 60.

I had finally figured out that most leaders struggle because we can't seem to "get out of our own heads". We get stuck replaying past decisions, failures, and losses instead of taking the learning from those experiences and moving forward.

Mentoring dozens of younger entrepreneurs throughout my own 40 years of growing companies taught me the value of "two heads really are better than one" in most situations. So, it just made sense to focus the rest of my career on helping my tribe (entrepreneurial leaders) find their way out of the jungle of isolation and loneliness through the coaching process.

Now, after six years and over 8,000 hours of coaching conversations, I am convinced that at least for us leaders, loneliness is more of a choice than a requirement for success. Through our work together, my clients have learned to put past pain and mistakes in their proper place (experiential education) and free their minds and hearts to focus on future relationships and success. I'm not talking about magic or a bunch of psycho-babble, I'm saying that loneliness is the result of a lot of "limiting self-beliefs" including:

- I'm not smart enough
- I've never done this before
- I don't have the resources to succeed
- No one wants to follow my leadership
- I mess up everything I try to do

- No one cares about me
- I don't know the right people
- I didn't go to the right school
- All my romantic relationships fail
- Folks from my family never amount to anything

Henry Ford once said: "If you don't think you can - you are right!" Looking at this list of limiting self-beliefs we see several things causing:

- Negativity—When we start with "NO" where do we go from there?
- Self-Focus—When we focus only on ourselves, we lock the door to outside support.
- Backward Looking—There is no "future in the past" only learning and moving forward.
- Finality—If I haven't succeeded so far, I never will. Who says?
- Pride—Yes pride—I'm too proud to accept input from others.
- Generalization—Saying every, always, never; instead, consider saying many, often, sometimes.
- Limited Resources—Keep looking, get creative, don't stop until someone says yes.

In the coaching process, I help leaders "deconstruct" these self-limiting beliefs to replace them with constructive learnings that will turn around the momentum in their personal and professional lives. As failure decreases and opportunities open up, they begin to become re-acquainted with the skills and talents that have lain dormant for so long. The excitement of even minor new successes is enough to fuel a whole new mindset and enthusiasm for winning.

If by now you are thinking; "That's all well and good Tony, but just talking to a coach is not going to heal my broken marriage" or "The alcohol and drugs have robbed me of everything I ever loved" or "I am so depressed I just don't have the energy to figure my life out", stay with me.

Coaching is only one tool that can help combat loneliness. Jane and I are also certified Biblical Counselors and use that training when working through difficult issues with married couples. While we often don't have any control over where we come from, who has impacted our lives for better or worse, or the resources we have to lead with, we do have choices!

The first choice we make when it comes to ending our loneliness is to start! Start believing there is a better path forward. Start believing we can surround ourselves with employees, co-leaders, and friends who can restore purpose and meaning to our efforts. Start thinking more of others than ourselves as a way to get out of our own way. Start focusing on the future and not the past.

Start allowing God to show you that you are never, ever truly alone!

Growing Forward

Take some time this week to consider the condition of your important relationships. Evaluate how much time and effort you are putting into maintaining and growing them. Then, set aside time each week to make a call, send an encouraging note or have coffee or share a meal with the important people in your life. Remember, leadership is a lonely endeavor. Guard your heart and your future by protecting these valuable relationships.

Treasure This

"David also said to Solomon, his son, "Be strong and courageous, and do the work. Do not be afraid or discouraged, for the LORD God, my God, is with you. He will not fail you or forsake you until all the work for the service of the temple of the LORD is finished."
1 Chronicles 28:20, NIV

"Loneliness and the feeling of being unwanted is the most terrible poverty."
Mother Teresa

"I've also seen that great men are often lonely. This is understandable, because they have built such high standards for themselves that they often feel alone. But that same loneliness is part of their ability to create."
Yousuf Karsh

52

Celebration

///

Take Time to Remember and Reward Success

It was finally time to go. After fourteen years as founders and co-owners of Salon Support, Inc., we were leaving for good. A few days earlier, my wife Jane and I had signed the sales documents making Salon Support a part of another company in our industry.

But in the last moments of that last day, as I grasped the door handle to leave for the last time, something happened and I will never forget. Allow me to provide a little background.

Salon Support, Inc. was my sixth company and the first to allow me to use many of the tools my former mentors had taught me. It was launched on a "shoestring" budget of $40,000 in 1994 and did a meager $163,000 in sales its first year (eventually it grew to over $18 million). The company's main focus was to provide lotion products and replacement tanning beds and lamps to retail stores in the indoor tanning and spa industry.

After running SSI for about 18 months, I was asked by the Mayor of Fort Worth to take over the Fort Worth Business Assistance Center—our new one-stop-shop for helping entrepreneurs start their own businesses. I convinced Jane to take over the company and then went on to grow the BAC.

While my tenure at the BAC was only supposed to last for one year, I ended up being there for about twenty-eight months. Next, the Kauffman Foundation recruited me to become an Entrepreneur-in-Residence, which kept me away for another five years. When I finally found my way back to Salon Support, Jane had turned our little company into an industry powerhouse. She had incorporated a state-of-the-art computer/telephone system, expanded our product offerings to over 1,800 SKUs, and created an annual full-color catalog that went out to over 20,000 retailers nationwide.

To say I was amazed at how the company had grown under Jane's leadership would be a total understatement. But the most impressive thing was the growth in the culture of the company. Every single employee had benefited from Jane's unique ability to blend high growth with a highly nurturing environment. Now my job was to help her and the team keep a good thing growing!

From the early days of setting up SSI, we knew that in order to attract the kind of high-quality talent we needed, our culture would have to be uniquely positive. I decided to make having fun and celebrating success a high priority. To this end, we began installing habits and traditions to make having fun a routine part of life at SSI.

Here are some of the things that made it a hoot to be a part of our team:

- Ringing the bell—When our sales reps completed their training and were ready to take their seat on the sales floor, they were each given a "hotel bell." Every time they got a sale, they would hit their bell, and the entire sales room would erupt in thunderous applause, hoots, and cheers. Eventually, our computer system was set up to allow each rep to have their own unique chime on the PA that sounded each time they entered a sale into the system. Even so, most of the veterans kept their bells and chose to celebrate "old school."

• Testifying—Every morning during our 15-minute sales meeting, the reps had an opportunity to share a testimony about methods and tools that were really working for them. Many routinely chose to give credit to one of their teammates for having given them the idea or freely sharing their best practices.

• Contests, Contests, Contests—Smart, aggressive people get bored very quickly. In order to keep things lively on the sales floor, we always had at least a few contests going simultaneously. While many contests rewarded outstanding prospecting, new account creation, or high volume and high margin sales efforts, it was how we awarded the prizes that kept things exciting. Every prize was awarded in public with everyone present. Along with money, we gave away televisions, vacation cruises, preferred parking spaces, movie tickets, gift certificates, weekend getaways, etc. But by far, the contest guaranteed to create the most buzz was always the "Win the chance to Pie the Leaders" sweepstakes. This contest ran for a month and allowed 10 lucky winners to bombard me, Jane, and our senior management team with whipped cream pies. It was great fun for everyone (but kind of hard to get out of our noses and ears).

• Playing Together—Each year, we would take a full day to celebrate our successes as a team. We would start the day with a company-wide overview of the previous year's successes, complete with graphs illustrating our growth in each department. Next was our "academy awards" ceremony, where 15-20% of our staff and management would be recognized with award trophies and monetary prizes for their outstanding contributions to Salon Support. Then, it was off to the race track, or bowling alley, or video arcade for several hours of hearty competition. These fun days bonded our people together in a very special way.

So, on that last day, knowing I was leaving this unique and wonderful culture made those last moments at Salon Support really tough. When I had finally mustered up the courage to walk out, I was really surprised to hear my name called out over the din of the sales floor.

"Hey Tony!" came the voice behind me. When I turned around, there stood Debbie, one of our veteran sales reps (all 4'10" of her). She stood looking up at me with her arms extended out, holding a bell. But this was no ordinary bell. It was the huge brass hotel bell our reps had given me on our 10th anniversary. I had simply forgotten to pick it up from the salesroom.

As I reached down to take it from her hands, the entire building exploded into a symphony of bell ringing, cheers, cat calls and applause. It was our last celebration together. It went on and on and with each ensuing new round of applause, my tears continued to drip down my quivering cheeks. But these tears were not borne of sadness. They were tears of gratitude as I left this incredible group of people better than I had found them. They were tears celebrating the wonderful joy we had discovered through the years of battling together to become the best we could be—as a team.

These days as I write and speak to so many new people, I often think back to those last moments at Salon Support.

I thank God that we had the opportunity to be a part of such a joyful celebration!

Growing Forward

In the everyday hustle and bustle of keeping things running, it is easy to overlook the importance of celebrating. Take a few minutes this week and ask yourself the question: How often and how well do we celebrate the wins (big and small) in our company? Then, jot down some ways to improve. I have never seen a company that celebrates its victories too much!

Treasure This

"For seven days celebrate the festival to the LORD your God at the place the LORD will choose. For the LORD your God will bless you in all your harvest and in all the work of your hands, and your joy will be complete."
Deuteronomy 16:15, NIV

"The most beautiful things are not associated with money; they are memories and moments. If you don't celebrate those, they can pass you by."
Alek Wek

"Celebrate your successes. Find some humor in your failures."
Sam Walton

Coaching Clients Comments

"Tony is at his best sitting down in one-to-one coaching sessions. He brings decades of experience and a generous heart for helping others get unstuck from what holds them back. This was acknowledged by his business owner peers, as Tony was named BOARD MEMBER OF THE YEAR multiple times. Tony makes the time to give back to others, especially those in greatest need."

Valerie and Ed Riefenstahl
The Alternative Board | Owners

"Since investing in my coaching relationship with Tony my entire life has improved. My business has grown, and I finally feel like the owner instead of an employee of the business. I am experiencing more freedom and I'm totally enjoying life. Most importantly though I'm a better husband and a better father. My family experiences me as the person God knows me to be instead of a hurried, and much more impatient version of me. I'm absolutely loving life. Thank you, Tony!"

Michael Moore
M3 Networks | President and CEO

"Tony was, and remains to be, an enormous part of the re-birth of our business. After 9 years of stagnant business practices that were not necessarily in our best interest, Tony opened our eyes to the overall disconnect. He made us see that "agreement, respect, and kindness" is the most critical recipe for success, professionally and personally. We would highly recommend his coaching services to anyone needing a wake-up call, encouragement, "straight shooting" advice, or helpful tips to ensure one's success."

Joanne & Nathan Weber
T & P Tavern | Proprietors

Coaching Clients Comments

"Tony opened my eyes not only to the deficiencies within my business but also helped me understand that 'When you set it up right, it runs right!' His wisdom and insight along with his unwavering honesty has brought about a new self-awareness; helping me accelerate the growth of my business and even my personal life. Being coached by this incredible man has given me something invaluable – a "true blessing" to my company, relationships, and life. I'm eternally grateful for Tony Ford!"

Corey Sands
BHM Entertainment | Vice President

"Tony operates consistently with honesty and integrity, and I'm thankful for the time and effort he devoted to me, my family, our team, and our companies.
To successfully engage the decisions and trials our teams were facing, I was in need of a confident, capable and willing mentor. Tony was just that, and his attitude was all in. He has encouraged me, coached me, counseled me, and lifted me and my family in prayer. He has provided both personal and professional wisdom; each of those easily crossing over into the other. During the year and a half Tony spent with us, many goals were realized and exceeded along with the residual overflow into other areas."

Jon Pastusek
XS Sight Systems | CEO

"Tony Ford is so much more than a business coach. I come away from sessions with him armed with tools and resources that not only make me a better business leader and entrepreneur, but a better person overall. Working with Tony helps me refine my thinking, discover my blind spots to challenge my biases, and learn to better utilize my resources."

Nneka Ejere
Pharmacist & "Survivor" Participant

d8d1c2f6-122e-403c-acb2-014f64db16b4R01